It's not fair - or is it?

a guide to developing children's ideas
through primary science enquiry

Written and edited by

Jane Turner, Brenda Keogh, Stuart Naylor and Liz Lawrence

With contributions from

The ASE Primary Science Committee

Millgate House Education

The **Association**
for **Science Education**
Promoting Excellence in Science Teaching and Learning

First published 2011 by Millgate House Publishers and Association for Science Education

Millgate House Publishers is an imprint of

Millgate House Education Ltd,

30 Mill Hill Lane,

Sandbach,

CW11 4PN, UK

Association for Science Education

College Lane

Hatfield

AL10 9AA, UK

Typesetting and Graphic Design by Kathryn Stawpert

Illustrations by Ged Mitchell

Printed and bound in Great Britain by Crewe Colour Printers.

ISBN 978-0-9562646-0-2

British Library Cataloguing in Publication Data

A catalogue record for this book is available from the British Library.

Acknowledgements

Like most publications, this book draws on contributions from several sources. These include:

- Ged Mitchell: illustrations

- Kathryn Stawpert: graphic design

- Joanna Williams: project management

- teachers and children, especially those from Sandbach Community Primary School, the Wroxham School, Potters Bar and Valley Primary School, Bromley who contributed ideas and provided examples of science enquiries

- members of the ASE Primary Science Committee, who provided valuable ideas and expertise at the early stages, which were taken forward by the original working group of Debbie Eccles, Anne Goldsworthy, Liz Lawrence, Kathy Schofield, Jane Turner and Nancy Bilderbeck. All Primary Science Committee members continued to generously offer constructive support and insights throughout the writing and editing process.

Jane Turner, Brenda Keogh, Stuart Naylor & Liz Lawrence

Millgate House Education and Association for Science Education, April 2011

Contents

Introduction

HOW TO USE THIS BOOK

This book is about science enquiry. It describes different types of science enquiry, how they help with developing understanding and how children's scientific enquiry skills develop. It is for all primary teachers and student teachers who want to know more about science enquiry and how to teach it, and for subject leaders who want to lead science effectively in their schools.

It has been written to help you broaden the range of science enquiries that your children experience, beyond Fair Testing to other important types of science enquiry, including Observing over Time, Identifying and Classifying, Pattern Seeking and Research.

This book can help you to answer the following questions:

> **How will I stimulate the children to explore as a lead in to science enquiry?**
> Purposeful science enquiry happens when children are motivated to answer a question that matters to them. What questions or problems will lead to children engaging in enquiry?

> **What will children do?** What kind of activities will help them use different types of science enquiry to develop a range of science concepts? What opportunities are there for them to develop their skills in predicting, planning, observing, measuring, recording, communicating and evaluating?

> **How will I encourage children's talk and questions?** Children's talk and questions are central to their developing understanding in science. What opportunities will the children have to talk to each other and raise questions?

> **What outcomes am I looking for?** What kind of assessment evidence will be generated to help me feel confident that children are developing knowledge and skills from their experience?

There are **FIVE** main chapters. Each chapter covers a different type of science enquiry.

1. Observing over Time
2. Identifying and Classifying
3. Pattern Seeking
4. Research
5. Fair Testing

Each chapter includes TWO sections

SECTION 1 INTRODUCTION

Information about the type of science enquiry

> What is it?

> Why do it?

> Which science topics does it suit best?

Ways of getting children started

> What might children say or notice to begin this type of science enquiry?

> What things can you say or do to begin this type of science enquiry?

> What kinds of questions can children investigate using this type of science enquiry?

> What can children do in this type of science enquiry?

> What activities can they engage in to learn about different science concepts?

> What skills do they use?

> How can these skills be developed and extended?

How to encourage talk and questioning

> How can you respond to children's questions?

> What questions can you ask?

> What is your role in children's conversations?

Possible outcomes that will provide assessment evidence for you

> How can children record and communicate what they find out?

> What skills can children demonstrate and how?

> What knowledge and understanding do they show and how?

SECTION 2 EXAMPLES

Four activities are described in detail to exemplify the particular type of science enquiry at different stages:

> Foundation

> Early primary

> Middle primary

> Late primary

You can use this book to help you to plan for science, to review your planning or, if you have a monitoring role, to support and review other teachers' planning and the scheme of work for science by considering:

> Are all enquiry types included?

> Are certain types missing?

> Are the contexts appropriate and challenging?

Health and Safety Notes

- *We recommend ASE's Be Safe! (2011) for working safely with children when carrying out science activities. Specific guidance for Health and Safety is included for each activity. You should follow the guidance carefully.*

- *Some activities involve children working out of doors. It is essential that you follow your school guidelines fully. Useful guidance about working out of doors is provided in Be Safe! p12-14. Guidance about hand washing is provided on p11.*

WHAT IS SCIENCE ENQUIRY?

Teachers can have different kinds of activities in mind when they refer to science enquiry in primary classrooms. Some view science enquiry as discovery learning, while others see working systematically as fundamental; some assume that it's only about practical work, while others feel that it should include children learning scientific concepts.

Our view is that

> **science enquiry is what children do in order to answer scientific questions about the world around them.**

We see them doing this by asking questions, collecting and analysing data, developing explanations and solving problems. They use these science enquiry skills in a variety of contexts, seeking evidence to test their ideas and answer questions. For example, sorting materials to find out which are magnetic, observing how a snowman melts, researching where milk comes from, looking for patterns in plant growth, or investigating how a ball bounces on different floor surfaces. It is the search for evidence to answer scientific questions that makes these different activities science enquiry.

There are several ways in which children can collect and analyse evidence. However,

> **surveys show that in many primary schools science enquiry generally means doing a fair test**

so children's experience of other types of science enquiry is limited. This book attempts to redress the balance.

Fair tests are the best way to answer many questions, such as:

> › Does sugar dissolve faster in hot tea?

> › Which is the best paper for wrapping fish and chips?

> › How warm does it have to be before our lettuce seeds start to germinate?

However there are other situations where fair testing isn't appropriate. These include:

> › investigating things that can't be changed or controlled, such as where daisies grow on a field

> › monitoring changes over time, such as how a puddle evaporates

> › finding out about complex systems, such as the water cycle or how the circulatory system works.

In these situations other types of science enquiry are required. Children can't use a fair test to answer these questions.

> **Different types of questions and situations require different types of enquiry**

so children and teachers need a repertoire to choose from. This book is called **It's not fair – or is it?** because it emphasises the other types of science enquiry, as well as fair testing. It draws on earlier work carried out in the AKSIS Project (Goldsworthy, Watson and Wood Robinson, 2000), in which some of these other types of science enquiry were characterised and exemplified. The types of science enquiry described in separate chapters in this book are:

> **Observing over Time:** children observe or measure how one variable changes over time

> **Identifying and Classifying:** children identify features or tests that help them to distinguish between different things

> **Pattern Seeking:** children observe and record phenomena, carry out surveys or collect data from secondary sources, and then identify relationships between the data in their findings

> **Research:** children use secondary sources of evidence to answer their questions

> **Fair Testing:** children identify the effect of changing one variable on another, whilst attempting to keep other variables constant.

Each chapter gives an overview of that type of enquiry and four detailed illustrations at different age ranges. For each type of enquiry, the process will normally follow a sequence similar to this:

Exploring	Children explore a question, statement, problem, idea, artefact, living thing or event as a starting point to enquiry.
Collecting and analysing evidence	Children observe over time, look for patterns, identify and classify, research using secondary sources or carry out a fair test, and record and analyse their findings.
Reaching a suitable and satisfying outcome	Children solve a problem, answer a question, develop an explanation, make and evaluate an artefact or system, provide evidence to justify why the outcome is appropriate, or raise more questions to investigate.

Each stage of the sequence is important. Children's experience of science can often focus on collecting and recording evidence. The initial stage of exploring, and the final stage of evaluating and justifying outcomes, can often be overlooked.

The enquiry types included here are those that children use to test ideas and collect evidence about the world around them. Although problem solving is not an enquiry type in itself, it is an important starting point for science enquiry. Solving a problem provides a purpose and creates a context for science enquiry.

Similarly, aspects of technology can provide an engaging purpose and context for children's science activities. They can also be a means of solving a science enquiry problem, or the outcome of a science enquiry problem. These are valuable in the classroom as well as in the real world. For example, making a boat provides a purposeful context for exploring floating and sinking. Children can use their technological skills to solve a scientific problem, such as making a parachute in order to work out what size parachute different people will need. They can apply their science knowledge and understanding in a design technology task, such as using an electrical circuit in a torch.

The importance of exploring

> **A period of exploration is a really valuable lead in to more systematic enquiry**

especially when learners encounter objects or events for the first time. We see this with children at a water tray, where initially they aren't interested in working out carefully which things float and which things sink. They just want to throw all the objects into the tray and play with them for a bit! It's much easier to get them to work more carefully and systematically after a period of exploration.

We use the term exploring to describe the period of unstructured finding out that goes on at the beginning of many science enquiries. Exploring objects, events and ideas can be the start of the enquiry process, and this book contains lots of ideas for starting points that provoke curiosity. **Exploration may happen spontaneously**, when children are intrigued by objects or events and want to find out more. More often in school,

> **exploration will be stimulated by questions or problems that you pose, interesting objects that you provide or events that you plan.**

Your task as a teacher is to find a 'hook' that will make an interesting starting point, inspiring children to find out more about the science that you want them to learn.

If children are going to genuinely explore, then they need plenty of interesting things, ideas and problems to stimulate them. Children need to engage with real things that they can handle, as well as ideas; they need to explore both inside and outside the classroom; they need plenty of time to do this exploring; and they need to talk with each other and with adults about what they discover.

An environment that encourages curiosity, creativity, exploration and inventiveness will result in children making lots of interesting observations and asking plenty of challenging questions. You should value and use these questions and ideas. You can help children to refine their questions, leading them to more focused activity where evidence is collected more systematically and analysed in greater depth.

The importance of progression

> **The science enquiry process is essentially the same whatever the age and maturity of the children, but the skills that they use when doing science enquiry should develop as they move through school.**

There is a progression in the skills they need to develop in order to carry out increasingly complex and challenging enquiries. To help you plan for and monitor this progression of science skills, in each chapter there are brief progression charts of the skills that children use when carrying out the different types of science enquiry.

We have used a straightforward model for describing how children's skills in science enquiry develop:

› Children become increasingly **autonomous** in their decision making and activity

› Children become increasingly **systematic** and **accurate** in their collecting and analysing of evidence

› Children increasingly build on **scientific ideas** in their predictions and explanations.

This progression of science enquiry skills depends on children being given opportunities to use their skills in contexts that are appropriate and challenging. You can help them to do this by ensuring that they progress:

› from investigating **simple** ideas to more **complex** or **abstract** ideas

› from investigating **familiar** things and experiences to **unfamiliar** things and experiences

› from investigating **concrete** things that they can see, hold and manipulate to things that are too **small, large, faraway** or **abstract** to see, hold and manipulate.

How will you decide what type of enquiry children will do?

> **If you know about the different types of enquiry, then you can build this into your planning. If children know about the different types of enquiry, then they can make decisions about which approach will be best in different circumstances.**

Although you don't need to plan a certain number of each type of enquiry every year, it is valuable for children to engage with all the different types regularly. As they get older, children should make choices about what type of enquiry they need to do in order to answer questions or solve problems. This book can help you to plan for this.

Types of enquiry

OBSERVING OVER TIME I Introduction

What is Observing over Time?

Observing over time helps us to identify and measure events and changes in living things, materials and physical processes and events. These observations may take place over time spans from minutes or hours (e.g. puddles evaporating, or watching a shadow move) to several weeks or months (e.g. growing plants, or hatching eggs and rearing the young chicks).

Observing over time provides opportunities for children to be actively involved in making decisions about what and how to observe and measure, and the best ways to record the changes that occur. It also provides relevant contexts for predicting. As patterns emerge in the observations, children can make predictions about what will happen next or re-evaluate predictions they made at the start of their enquiry.

Some observing over time enquiries help children to develop their understanding of natural sequences of events, such as germination and growth, or the phases of the Moon. Other enquiries allow them to look for simple explanations, such as why sound levels in the classroom change during the day. These types of enquiries provide rich contexts for children to learn about the importance of cycles, systems, growth and decay, and other types of changes. They link readily with activities in other curriculum areas, especially design and technology, mathematics and English.

The table on the next page shows a wide range of starting points for observing over time.

Getting started

Opportunities for observing over time arise where children are able to look at things that change, such as the length and position of shadows during the day, ice melting, plants coming into flower, bread going mouldy, and tadpoles turning into frogs.

Children may make observations and raise questions spontaneously, based on their own curiosity and exploration of the world around them. However not all observing over time activities will be initiated by children. You can also encourage children to notice things that change over time. Fascinating objects, everyday items seen in close-up, living things, news stories, fictional stories and events in the local environment can all lead in to relevant and stimulating observing over time enquiries. You can also present children with a problem that requires them to observe something changing over time.

Observing change over time often leads to other types of investigations. These include **fair testing** to see whether and how changing different variables can affect how something changes; **pattern seeking** to identify a correlation between changes and other factors; **classifying** to find out whether species or materials change in the same way; and **research** using secondary sources to find out more about the changes observed.

Starting points for Observing over Time

LIVING THINGS

Changes in animals

The frogspawn has turned into frogs. How do animals change from eggs or babies to adults? (e.g. cats humans, frogs, butterflies, chicks, sheep)

What changes? (e.g. appearance, movement, sound, diet)

How quickly do they grow?

Animal movement

The snail's body ripples when it moves, and it goes really slowly. How far will it go in five minutes? Do other animals move faster or slower?

If we watch an insect or a bird for a few minutes, where does it go and how far does it move?

Seasonal change

The leaves on the big tree by the gate have gone red but these haven't. How do different trees change in the spring / summer / autumn / winter?

They've just cut the grass on the school field. How does it change as it starts to grow again? How do ponds or other habitats change over the year? (e.g. in appearance or in the wildlife visiting it)

Growing plants

I've got some bean seeds. I think they might grow like in Jack and the Beanstalk. How do our seeds change as they germinate? How long do they take to germinate? How do plants change as they grow?

Which are the quickest plants for us to grow to eat? How long does it take us to grow a pumpkin for Halloween?

Compost

We're going to use vegetable scraps to make some compost. How will our compost heap change over time?

Ourselves

Here are the photos of all of us as babies. Don't we look different! How do we change as we get older? (e.g. body proportions, hair, height, weight, skills)

Microorganisms

I was going to use this bread for sandwiches but look what's happened! How does food change as it goes mouldy? (**Safety:** Do not use meat or fish)

MATERIALS AND THEIR USES

Ice and snow

It's snowing! How does the appearance of the snow change as it melts? How does the temperature of the snow change as it melts? How long does our snowball last?

What will happen to our snowman?

Rubbish

Our rubbish is separated into different types for recycling. How do things change over time if we bury them in the ground? Do all things rot? (**Safety:** Do not use meat or fish)

Bubbles

We've bought some bubble kits for the party. How long do our bubbles last?

Water evaporating

There's a huge puddle in the playground. What happens to it by lunchtime?

How quickly will this wet sponge dry so I can pack it in a suitcase?

If we dissolve salt in water we can get it back by evaporating the water. Does it work with other solids? How about sugar? Or flour?

Food

When we heat chocolate it melts. How does an egg change when we boil or scramble it? Or cheese when it is heated? Or bread when we toast it? Or popcorn when we heat it?

What happens to food when we leave it out? (e.g. bread going stale, crisps going soft).

How does the weight of food change as it dries?

FORCES, ENERGY AND MOVEMENT

Floating and sinking

Our sponge is lower in the water than it was. What happens to other things when we put them on top of the water? (e.g. paper, polystyrene, wood, sieve)

Movement

Let's look at things moving. Where do bubbles go when the wind blows?

EARTH AND SPACE

Sun and shadows

I noticed that my shadow was very long when I went home in the afternoon. How do our shadows change over a day?

Does the Sun rise and set at the same time every day?

What's the brightest or hottest part of the day?

Moon and stars

The Moon has changed from a disc to a banana shape. How does the Moon's appearance change over a month?

How do the positions of the stars in the sky change?

Weather

It was really chilly this morning and now it's really warm. How does the temperature change over the day / month / year?

Does the wind always blow from the same direction?

Rocks and soils

We can't read the words on the gravestones. Which ones are the hardest to read? Is it the oldest ones? How have they changed?

Do buildings and statues change in the same way? How can you tell?

SOUND

Noise

When is it noisiest in our classroom? When is it quietest?

When is it noisiest in the play area? When is it quietest?

LIGHT

Light levels

I think our classroom gets darker by lunchtime. How does the light level in our classroom change during the day?

What can children do when they observe over time?

Ideas for activities

There are many different contexts in which children can carry out observing over time enquiries. Some suggestions for these are given in the Starting Points table on the previous two pages, and in each of the four activities described in detail later.

Developing scientific skills and understanding

When there is something fascinating to watch, like a tadpole changing or a shrinking snowman, children can be keen and perceptive observers. The desire to find out what is happening provides a good incentive for them to observe what is changing. Observing over time enquiries that capture children's attention provide particularly good contexts for children to use and develop the skills of observing, measuring, recording and interpreting data (including using ICT). These skills provide a distinctive way for children to develop their understanding of scientific ideas. As children develop their skills, the depth and range of their understanding should also increase.

As in all types of scientific enquiry, children should become progressively more systematic and show more independence in the way they plan and carry out observing over time enquiries. Their observations and measurements should become more precise, moving from simple description to detailed observation and careful measurements. Children should become increasingly sophisticated in the way they interpret their observations and develop more complex explanations using a range of evidence. Their evaluation of their enquiries should also show an increased awareness of the effectiveness of their working methods.

Many enquiries of this type involve making qualitative observations that are likely to be recorded as a diary or log. These might be presented as a table, sequence or booklet of drawings, a set of photographs or a sequence of notes or annotations.

Where data are measured and collected over time there are opportunities for younger children to draw and interpret bar charts and explore simple ways of presenting the data. Older children will have opportunities to use more complex ways of presenting data. These will include constructing line graphs, where they can plot two continuous variables against each other (e.g. wind speed and rate of evaporation), read between the marked points, consider how the graph might continue and draw conclusions about how the variables are connected.

The grid on page 22 shows the progression of skills that children use when observing over time. You can use the grid to ensure that there is sufficient challenge in the observing over time enquiries you plan.

Encouraging talk and questioning

A fascinating object like a melting ice hand or a hatching chick will get children talking. That is the easy bit! Children make lots of observations of the world that they experience, but these don't necessarily lead to scientific enquiriy. You can encourage children to turn their observations into questions by reflecting their observations back to them, inviting suggestions for possible activities.

Josh says the shadow has moved. Is he right? Has the shadow moved? How can we be sure? Talk to your partner about your ideas.

You might want to narrow the focus of children's observations to help them identify one feature to observe.

You have all noticed so many ways in which the chicks are changing – the way they move, their feathers, the amount they eat . . . there are so many things to observe! Shall we do one thing each?

You might indicate the sort of skills or equipment they could use.

Could we count the number of leaves on the plant? What can we use to measure how tall the plant has grown?

Sometimes your task will be to help the children recognise that there are things happening that they didn't expect or notice. More careful observation is required to really know what is happening.

Are you sure that all the fruit has gone mouldy? Which went mouldy first?

Giving children time to talk to each other about what they have noticed will encourage them to turn their initial observations into questions that can be investigated practically. With your support, they can make decisions about what changes to observe and how to measure and record these changes.

What are the possible outcomes?

Observing over time enquiries will lead to outcomes that will provide rich assessment evidence:

> detailed descriptions of changing objects, systems and phenomena, in word, picture and numerical formats

> the development of scientific understanding about concepts such as change and growth

> children being able to think, talk and write about the skills they have used

> explanations of the changes they observed linking their findings to their scientific knowledge.

Observing over Time : Skills Progression Grid

	Plan	Do	Review
Foundation	• I am curious about things that change • With help I ask questions about things changing • I talk about my ideas for finding out how things change	• I use all my senses to observe changes • I look closely at how things change • I make simple records of how things change (with help where necessary) • I use simple equipment to observe and record changes	• I talk about what I have done and what I noticed
Early primary	• I ask questions about how and why things change • With help, I identify changes to observe and measure and suggest how to do it	• I use non-standard units and simple equipment to record changes • I record in words or pictures, or in simple prepared formats such as tables and charts	• I identify simple changes and talk about them • I sequence the changes • I begin to use scientific language to talk about changes • I talk about whether the change was what I expected
Middle primary	• I talk about things changing and decide when questions can be answered by observing over time • I decide what observations to make, how often and what equipment to use	• I use a range of equipment to collect data using standard measures • I make records using tables and bar charts • I begin to use and interpret graphs produced by dataloggers	• I draw simple conclusions from the changes I observed • I talk about changes using some scientific language • I suggest improvements to the ways I observe
Late primary	• I recognise when observing changes over time will help to answer my questions • I decide how detailed my observations need to be, and what equipment to use, to make my measurements as accurate as possible	• I use equipment accurately without support • I record data appropriately • I present data in line graphs • I interpret changes in the data • I recognise the effect of changing the time and number of observations	• I draw valid conclusions from data about changes • I recognise the significance of things changing over time • I talk about and explain changes using scientific knowledge and understanding • I evaluate how well I observed over time

HATCHING EGGS

It is easy to hire an egg hatching kit for the classroom. You can order fertilised eggs and an incubator and these are delivered a few days before the eggs are due to hatch. They are guaranteed to create an observing frenzy in the classroom! Soon after the eggs arrive, tiny fluffy chicks are scurrying around a small run and children are refusing to go out to play in case they miss something.

Make use of the high levels of motivation generated, and encourage this unstructured observation of the chickens as a starting point to more systematic observation. The children can chart the development of the chicks from egg to bird in a variety of ways, and begin to develop a rich first hand understanding of both growth and care for living creatures.

Health and Safety Notes
- *Children must wash their hands thoroughly if they handle the eggs or chickens.*
- *Clean surfaces of tables etc. with detergent if the chicks have been placed on them.*
- *Some children may be allergic to feathers.*
- *Check with the company providing the eggs that you have made appropriate arrangements for the welfare of the chicks during and after their stay.*

Getting started

You can build on children's spontaneous observations and questions

Children might be looking at books or pictures of birds' eggs in nests, or there may be a bird's nest that you can see from your classroom.

Look, the bird has come back to its nest. Are there eggs in the nest? What's inside the eggs?

I found an egg shell in my garden. Grandma said a baby bird came out of it.

I watched a programme about a baby bird coming out of an egg.

You can ask questions to focus their observations

It is likely that many children's experience of eggs will be confined to the kitchen. They may not make the connection between the eggs that they eat and the arrival of baby birds.

Where have you seen eggs? Do they look like the egg shell that you found in your garden?

What do you think might be inside the eggs in the nest? Have you seen baby birds? I have an idea about how we can find out more.

You can provide your own starting points

Usually this will start with a planned activity, since you need to organise delivery of the eggs and space and time to care for them. Observing will happen over time and all the time – this is not an activity that you can limit to a 40 minute lesson! It is almost impossible to predict all the things that children will notice, so be prepared to respond to their questions and observations with suggestions for how they can find out more in a safe way and without harming the chicks.

Mother hen has laid too many eggs. She can't look after them all. Can we help her?

Look what's arrived in school! I wonder what will happen to them?

WHAT CAN CHILDREN DO?

IDEAS FOR ACTIVITIES

Children can:

> think about how to care for the chicks and take turns in feeding and holding them gently

> simply sit and watch the chicks and talk about what they see happening

> think about what the chicks might look like when they are grown, and look at images of hens and cockerels

> with support, create a chick diary with written descriptions, annotated drawings and photographs

> create a class wall display showing the way that chicks change, using drawings, photographs, paintings and collage

> play a sequencing card game with images of the chick at different stages

> create a dance to reflect the movement of a chick, to a suitable sound or musical stimulus

> make models of chicks, choosing suitable materials to represent the way a chick looks and feels

> use their knowledge to talk to each other about caring for young animals as they develop

> visit someone who keeps hens.

DEVELOPING SKILLS AND UNDERSTANDING

Give children lots of opportunities to:

> ask questions about the eggs and what happens when the eggs hatch

> observe the chicks closely and talk about what they notice, (e.g. the sounds they make, what they feel like, their smell)

> record their observations in drawings, models or photographs

> compare what they have seen to what they know about other young animals

> talk about what happened to the eggs and how the chicks have changed

> use and develop key vocabulary (e.g. egg, chick, hatch, baby, adult, grow, change, feathers, down, feeding).

Encouraging talk and questioning

Encourage children to think about questions that can't be answered simply by observing the chicks.

Do you think there are chicks inside the eggs now? What do you think they look like? Do you think they can move around in there? What do you think they eat inside the egg? Are they alive? How do you think the chicks will get out? Where is their mummy? How will we look after them and make sure we keep them safe?

Help the children to use what they can see to talk to each other about what is happening.

Let's talk about the chickens. I've got some questions to get us thinking.

What happened to the egg? Which part of the chick did we see first? What did it do when it came out? Could it walk? What did it look like? Was it hungry?

Encourage the children to talk about what they could do to keep a record of the chicks' growth.

You've noticed lots of things about the chickens, but how do you think we can record some of our ideas? We've got cameras, we can draw, we can make a video. There are lots of things you can do. Talk with your partner about what you can do together.

Give the children plenty of time to talk with each other about what they have found out, and encourage them to tell visitors to the classroom about the changes they have seen. They may need to work in small groups, with support, to do this, but give them time to talk about their ideas first.

What's the most exciting thing that happened? What were the best things that you saw?

Mr Shah is visiting us this afternoon. He doesn't know much about chickens. Why don't you decide what you would most like to tell him? Perhaps he will have some new questions for us to answer.

What are the possible outcomes?

Observing chicks over time leads to different kinds of outcomes

These can provide rich assessment evidence of children's developing skills and understanding.

For example:

> what they say to you, and each other, about the similarities and differences between the chicks as they grow

> how they identify and describe different features of the chicks

> their annotated drawings and photographs of chicks, and other physical recordings of their observations

> their contribution to the chick diaries or wall display

> how they complete the sequencing card game

> the ideas they share through creating their dance

> their models of chicks and how they describe what they have made

> the ways that they compare the chicks with other animals

> the ideas that they suggest for how to care for the chicks.

Abigail said that the chicks' legs grow longer as they get older

Questions that can lead to other types of enquiry

Questions that children may ask (or you could ask them)

Do other animals grow faster or slower than chicks?

Do any other animals hatch from eggs?

Do other animals have feathers?

I wonder what chicks eat? How much do they eat?

Can they fly? How big do they get? When do they stop being chicks? Are they 'boy' or 'girl' chicks?

How do other animals grow?

How can you add challenge?

Children can be encouraged to:

> decide what features to observe and suggest how

> observe the chicks more systematically, making observations at regular intervals (e.g. movement, feeding)

> collect measured data, such as the height of the chicks

> consider how quickly the chicks grow and compare this to other living things (e.g. humans, dogs, sunflowers).

PUDDLES

Most children love splashing in puddles. Encouraging children to explore puddles lets us capitalise on their interest and point it in a scientific direction. When the rain has stopped, gradually shrinking puddles make an excellent focus for observing over time. Children become aware of puddles getting smaller and eventually disappearing without having to consciously observe what is happening.

To make their observations more scientific they can measure a puddle's changing size over a few hours, record the data, and begin to understand what happens when water evaporates and how different factors affect how quickly puddles change. Giving children time to explore water and puddles first will help them to raise questions and think about ideas and ways to investigate.

> ### *Health and Safety Notes*
> - *Make sure that children use appropriate footwear and clothing.*
> - *Make sure that children are supervised if they are walking in deep puddles.*
> - *Ensure that you follow the school's guidelines for working with children outdoors.*

Getting started

You can build on children's spontaneous observations and questions

Children notice when it's raining and when there are puddles on the ground. Rain and puddles make a big difference to whether they can play outside and where they can play.

There were puddles to splash in this morning. Where have they all gone? We don't need our wellies any more!

The big puddle by the fence has been there for days, but it's almost gone away now.

You can ask questions to focus their observations

Get the children to focus on how the puddles are changing.

Are the puddles the same size as they were earlier? Are they bigger or smaller?

Look at that big puddle. Do you think it will still be there when we come out to play later?

You can provide your own starting points

You can use observations or stories.

Look at this big puddle! I wonder if it will still be there later. Perhaps we could draw round it with chalk so we know exactly where it is. We can find out if it changes or if it stays the same.

One day Minnie and Mel found a huge puddle in the playground. They loved the puddle. They put on their wellies and raincoats and splashed in it. The next morning they rushed into school to play in the puddle. Oh no......

WHAT CAN CHILDREN DO?

IDEAS FOR ACTIVITIES

Children can:

> explore puddles by wearing wellies to walk or splash in the water

> talk and write about the best ways of observing and measuring how puddles change over time

> create their own puddles using shallow containers or plastic sheets

> add paint to puddles

> chalk lines round the puddles at different times, and use photos, videos or drawings to show how the puddles change, or mark the change of depth on wellington boots

> create paper cut outs of the changing shape and size of the puddle to use in a class display

> create a simple chart to show how puddles change

> create a poem or story about puddles

> talk to each other about what they think has happened to the puddles and what makes a difference to how they dry up

> think and talk about the possible connection between the puddles drying up and rain falling to make more puddles.

DEVELOPING SKILLS AND UNDERSTANDING

Give children lots of opportunities to:

> raise questions and suggest what they think will happen to puddles

> with support plan what to do (e.g. which puddles to measure, how to measure them, how often)

> try different methods of measuring how the puddles change in size and depth

> record what happens using writing, drawings, photos or videos

> relate their ideas to other experiences of water drying up (e.g. the floor after it's been washed)

> talk about whether the changes in the puddle were what they expected and why

> develop and use key vocabulary (e.g. water, puddle, bigger, smaller, drying up, rain, changing, deeper, shallower).

Encouraging talk and questioning

Encourage the children to play in the puddles and to share their observations. You can ask questions to direct their observations.

> Now that you have had a good splash let's have a think about the puddles. I've got some questions to help you. How big was the puddle when the rain stopped? Is it bigger or smaller now? Do you think it will change some more? What other things could we think about?

Encourage the children to think about the best way to observe the changes in the puddle. They may need some ideas to help them get started.

> How can we see if the puddle really does change? Talk to your partner about your ideas.
>
> Do you think we could draw a circle round it to see if it changes?
>
> Do you think we could see how high the water comes up your welly boot?
>
> Do you think we could use a measuring stick?

Encourage them to talk about what they have found out and to raise more questions.

> Talk to another group about what you found out. Did you find out the same things?
>
> I've got another question. I wonder what would happen if the puddle was on the playing field, not the playground?
>
> Here are some speech bubbles I've cut out for you. You can write your own questions in the speech bubbles.

Investigating puddles lays a foundation for later work on the water cycle. You can get them thinking about how evaporation and rain might be connected.

> I wonder where the water went to when the puddle dried up. What do you think?
>
> It feels like it's been raining for days! I wonder where all the water comes from to make the rain?

What are the possible outcomes?

Observing puddles over time leads to different kinds of outcomes

These can provide rich assessment evidence of children's developing skills and understanding.

For example:

> what they say to each other, and you, about how they explored the puddles and what happened

> what they want to record about the changes in the puddles

> photographs or drawings of how they investigated the puddles

> their annotated photographs, drawings and other records of how the puddles changed

> any descriptive or creative writing that they do about the puddles

> the content of their chart

> their descriptions of the changes in the puddles

> what they say about why they think puddles change

> what they say about how they observed and recorded, and ideas about what else they might have done.

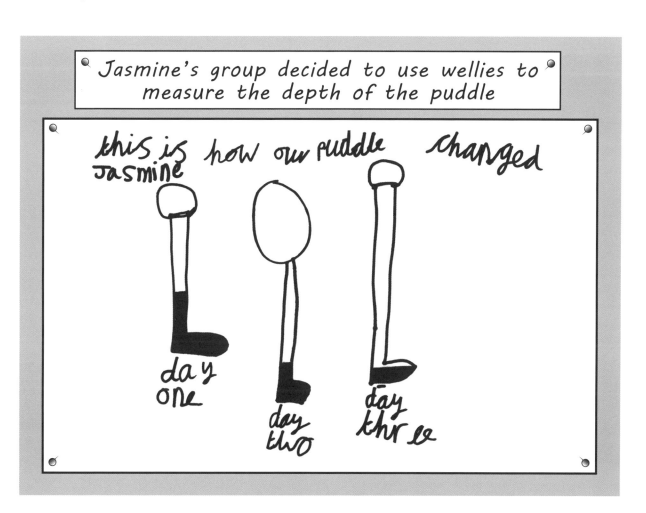

Jasmine's group decided to use wellies to measure the depth of the puddle

this is how our puddle changed

Jasmine

day one

day two

day three

Questions that can lead to other types of enquiry

Questions that children may ask (or you could ask them)

Some of the puddles are in the sunshine but others are in the shade. Does the sunshine make a difference to how quickly the puddle dries up?

I saw a programme about deserts last night. I wonder what it would be like living in a place where there isn't any rain?

Do the puddles all dry up at the same time?

Do deep puddles last longer than shallow ones?

How can you add challenge?

Children can be encouraged to:

> measure the rate of evaporation more accurately, using string to record the changing circumference or metre sticks to measure the depth of puddles

> present their data in a table or a bar chart

> consider what factors might have affected how quickly the puddle disappeared

> set up a test to investigate some of these other factors

> suggest further questions to investigate.

SHADOWS

Shadows make a good context for observing over time, though you do need a sunny day to make decent observations! As always, give children plenty of time to explore shadows before they start to ask more focused questions and think about investigating more systematically by observing over time.

Children can use a variety of objects to make a shadow in the classroom or playground. They can measure shadows at regular intervals and record the data. As they do they will learn more about the nature of shadows and how shadows change in predictable ways during the day. This will help them begin to understand the connection between the length and direction of the shadow and the movement of the Earth relative to the Sun.

> ### *Health and Safety Notes*
> - *Warn children about the dangers of looking directly at the Sun.*
> - *Follow the school's guidelines for working outdoors.*
> - *Ensure that children wear appropriate protection on sunny days.*

Getting started

You can build on children's spontaneous observations and questions

While children are playing in the playground they may notice differences in their shadows.

> *Your shadow makes your head look a funny shape!*
>
> *Look how big my shadow is!*

You can ask questions to focus their observations

You do not need to be outside to encourage children to think more about their shadows.

> *Can you always see your shadow?*
>
> *Does your shadow always look like that?*
>
> *What was your shadow like when you walked to school this morning?*

You can provide your own starting points

You can plan in advance to use shadows as a starting point for observing over time.

> *Can you jump on someone's shadow? Let's play shadow tag and catch each other's shadows.*
>
> *I'm sure my car was in the shade of the school hall when I parked it yesterday morning, but when I got in it later the Sun was shining on it and it was really hot inside. Do you think the shadow could have moved?*

You can pose a problem that will require children to observe shadows over time and think about what they observe.

> *Is it better to play shadow tag at lunchtime or after school?*
>
> *My granny says that if she puts her sun lounger under a tree in the morning and sits there all day she won't get burnt. I'm not sure. What do you think?*

WHAT CAN CHILDREN DO?

IDEAS FOR ACTIVITIES

Children can:

> talk to each other about how they can find out more about shadows
> go outside to measure shadows, using cardboard cut outs or sticks to measure the changing shadows
> help a puppet character who is upset because s/he thinks that their shadow getting shorter means s/he must be shrinking
> play a guessing game to see if they can work out where, and how long, the shadow will be next time they go outside to look
> take photos of shadows of objects around the school at different times of the day, and describe how they have changed
> make a bar graph of paper strips of shadow length plotted against time intervals
> make a simple sundial
> suggest solutions to problems that draw on their understanding of how shadows change, such as why the time of day makes a difference to playing shadow tag, or where the teachers should park if they want to get in a cool car at home time.

DEVELOPING SKILLS AND UNDERSTANDING

Give children lots of opportunities to:

> raise questions about shadows and predict how they think the shadow will change
> plan how to measure the length and position of the shadow
> observe and measure the length and position of shadows
> record the shadow length in an appropriate way (e.g. scale diagram; table of shadow length against time; bar graph of paper strips)
> describe their findings to each other
> give simple explanations linking cause and effect (e.g. the Earth moves during the day, so the Sun shines from different directions)
> evaluate what they did (e.g. did we observe regularly, did we record accurately?)
> develop and use key vocabulary (e.g. shadow, Sun, light, Earth, dark, movement, angle, longer, shorter, changing, direction).

Encouraging talk and questioning

Encourage children to explore shadows and to raise their own questions:

 What have you noticed about shadows? I've started a list. Talk to your partner and see what you can add to the list.

A discussion about tactics in a game of shadow tag will provide good reasons for finding out when shadows are longer or shorter.

 We've had a great time playing shadow tag in the playground. Do you think that the time of day will make a difference? Have a chat with your partner about the best time to play shadow tag.

Children can be given the opportunity to think about how to observe shadows more systematically. You may need to suggest ways in which they could make and measure a shadow.

 How do we find out if shadows really do move and change? Could we use the football goalposts to help us? Talk together about what you could do to see if shadows change during the day.

When they have finished their observations, encourage them to talk about what they have found out and think of more questions.

 I wonder if you all found out the same things about shadows changing? Share your ideas with someone else. Do you agree?

I've got a question. Do you think that the shadows will be the same when we come back after the holiday?

I'll put my question on the question board. Can you add more questions?

What are the possible outcomes?

Observing shadows over time leads to different kinds of outcomes

These can provide rich assessment evidence of their developing skills and understanding.

For example:

> what they say to each other, and you, about how they observed the shadows and what they found out

> how they work together to solve the problems

> the drawings and other records they make when they are observing the shadows

> their bar graphs

> photographs of changing shadows, and the annotations they add to them

> their descriptions of the way the shadows change

> the way they use secondary sources to build up their understanding of changing shadows

> what they say about changing shadows and what they think causes the shadows to change

> their evaluation of the skills that they have used and the way that they investigated.

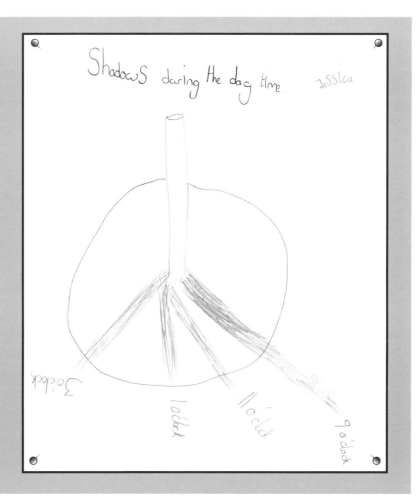

Jessica said that the shadows are shortest in the middle of the day because the Sun is higher in the sky

Questions that can lead to other types of enquiry

Questions that children may ask (or you could ask them)

How does a sundial work?
Can you get a shadow from something transparent like a glass of water?

What's the darkest shadow that you can make?
If I sit in the shade on a sunny day will I still get sunburn?

How can you add challenge?

Children can be encouraged to:

> present the shadow length data in a line graph

> make scale drawings of shadow length and position

> use a simple model (e.g. torch and stick) to show the relative positions of Sun and Earth and how this affects shadow length.

MOULD

As the name suggests, most microorganisms are too small to see with the naked eye. When lots of microorganisms are collected together in one place then they can become visible. Moulds are fascinating examples of microorganisms that can be observed easily in the classroom. Mould will grow readily on samples of bread, cheese and fruit in a warm classroom. Children can observe changes in the moulds over time, and go on to learn more about how microorganisms influence our daily lives.

A mould garden, using moist bread in a closed plastic bag that is punctured by a few pinpricks, can be used to show a variety of moulds. Alternatively, put the bread in a large screw-top jar with the lid fitted loosely.

Health and Safety Notes

- *Securely close (but do not seal) all containers in which microorganisms are grown. Do not uncover them for clearer observation. Dispose of the mouldy bread carefully, so that people don't come into contact with it. The unopened container can be placed in the school's normal refuse bin. Ensure that children and adults wash their hands thoroughly after handling the containers.*

- *Do not use fish or meat of any kind. Never allow fermentation by yeasts in sealed containers because the pressure of the gas generated could cause an explosion.*

- *Additional information can be found in ASE Be Safe! pages 16-17.*

Getting started

You can build on children's spontaneous observations and questions

Children will encounter moulds in a variety of contexts.

I forgot to take my lunch box home on Friday and my left over cheese sandwich has gone mouldy.

Mum saved some birthday cake for when my grandad came, but it was all furry when it came out of the box.

You can ask questions to focus their observations

Focus your questions on microorganisms that are safe to explore further.

Does bread or cake always go mouldy? How long do you think it takes? Are there ways of slowing it down? How could we find out?

You can provide your own starting points

You can make an observation.

When I came home from a weekend away the bread that I left in the bread bin had gone mouldy, but the loaf in the fridge was fine. I'm not sure why. Can you help me to find out?

WHAT CAN CHILDREN DO?

IDEAS FOR ACTIVITIES

Children can:

> think and talk about things that they have seen going mouldy and how they can monitor mould growth

> use a digital microscope to look closely at the moulds changing

> make detailed drawings of the changes, or create a sequence of annotated digital microscope images, mini videos or photos

> use small squared graph paper to measure the amount of mould

> draw line graphs, plotting the amount of growth against time

> find out more about mould growth using secondary sources

> create warning posters or leaflets about mould growth, or a guide to keeping food fresh

> create true-false statements about microorganisms for other children to use.

DEVELOPING SKILLS AND UNDERSTANDING

Give children lots of opportunities to:

> ask questions about how mould can be investigated (e.g. how fast does it grow?)

> plan how to grow mould safely and to record results systematically

> observe the mould closely (e.g. using a digital microscope or visualiser)

> take measurements and record how quickly the mould is growing (e.g. take photographs and describe the colour and texture of the mould. Shade in the equivalent area of mould on a scale diagram on squared paper. Plot the data on a line graph)

> describe what they have observed

> use their scientific knowledge to explain what they have observed and make predictions about mould growth in different conditions or on different foods

> evaluate how effective their investigation was and how they might improve it (e.g. did we measure at the right time intervals? Did we think about other factors that might have affected the rate of growth?)

> develop and use key vocabulary (e.g. mould, microorganisms, preserve, develop, change, spread, reproduce, spores, prevent).

Encouraging talk and questioning

Encourage children to think and talk about their experience outside school. Where and when have they seen things going mouldy? Do the situations have anything in common? Get them to talk about these problems and plan how they can investigate how mould grows.

You've all been thinking about things going mouldy. It's time to get together to share our ideas. Here are a couple of questions to get you started.

I wonder when the mould starts to grow?

Does it grow in just one place on the food or all over the food?

Help them to think about the questions they would like to research further and how to organise their observations to find the answers.

Let's grow some mould in the classroom. It will be in closed containers for safety.

You need to think about how to organise your observations. How can we measure it? How often should we measure it? How will we record any changes?

Encourage them to talk about what they have found out and think of new questions to explore.

You each observed different things. I want you to visit each other's tables and gather as much information as you can so that your group can put together a report. First you need to talk about what questions to ask each other.

You have found out lots of really interesting things. I've still got some questions. Does mould grow on all types of food? Does it grow more on some foods than others? Is it more dangerous on some types of food?

What are the possible outcomes?

Observing mould over time leads to different kinds of outcomes

These can provide rich assessment evidence of their developing skills and understanding.

For example:

> what they say to each other, and you, about how they will observe the mould growth and what they found out

> their drawings, photographs and other records of the changes

> the way that they measure the changes in mould growth using graph paper, line graphs and other recordings

> their descriptions of the changes in the moulds

> the language they use when they talk about moulds

> the content of their guide to food preservation

> the true-false statements that they create

> their warning poster, or guide to keeping food fresh

> their evaluations of the skills and processes they have used.

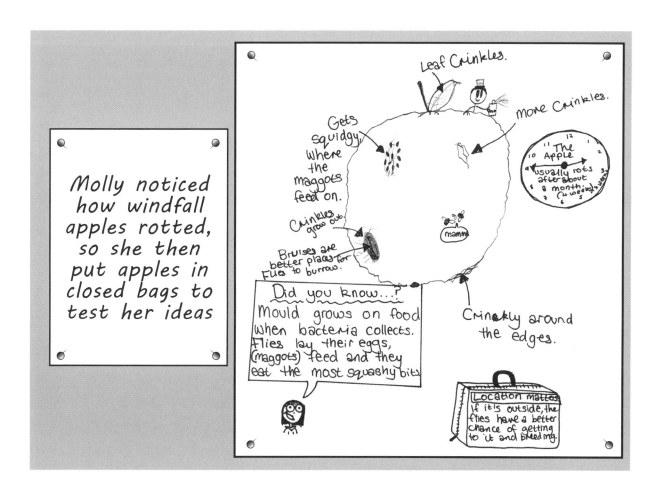

Molly noticed how windfall apples rotted, so she then put apples in closed bags to test her ideas

Questions that can lead to other types of enquiry

> I've seen mouldy bread, would mould on an apple look the same?
>
> Will all food go mouldy eventually?

Health and Safety Notes

- *Do not let children investigate mould grown on fish and meat. Questions such as this should be investigated using secondary sources.*

> What makes mould grow faster?
>
> How can we can stop food going mouldy?

How can you add challenge?

Children can be encouraged to:

> be more systematic in the collection of data (e.g. controlled environment, more precise measurements)

> compare rates of growth of mould on different foods and in different conditions

> find out how to slow down the growth of moulds.

IDENTIFYING AND CLASSIFYING I Introduction

What is Identifying and Classifying?

Identifying and classifying are key scientific activities that we engage in to help us make sense of how the world is organised. This happens intuitively, from a very early age. Very young children learn to recognise mum and dad, or big sister or brother, when they appear. They notice that all these people have different voices, and the family dog or cat sounds different again. They identify the sounds or smells that are made when food is being prepared, and they notice that different foods have different tastes, smells and textures. As they get older they begin to work out what things are by observing closely, learning the names of different things, noticing characteristics, similarities and differences, and learning how things are grouped together because of their characteristics.

Children develop these skills by sorting many different kinds of materials, objects and living things, and recognising that these can be classified using different criteria. For example, if they want to make a fridge magnet they need to understand that some things are magnetic, but this may not be a helpful characteristic if they want to make an umbrella. Deciding what these criteria should be helps to consolidate their skills. These types of enquiries provide valuable contexts for children to learn about the rich variety of living things, rock and soil types and materials. They link readily with activities in other curriculum areas, especially design and technology, mathematics, English and art.

The table on the next page shows examples of starting points for identifying and classifying.

Getting started

Opportunities for identifying and classifying arise in situations where children can identify that not all things are the same − birds, flowers, children, pens, and so on. Once they recognise this, they can use these differences to sort objects into groups and find new things that fit into those groups.

Children may make some connections spontaneously, based on their own questions about and observations of the world around them. However, not all identifying and classifying activities will be initiated by children. You can also encourage children to observe things carefully, systematically record differences and sort things into groups. These don't have to be unusual objects. Everyday items can often be really interesting when we look at them carefully with a classifying question in mind. For example, kitchen utensils can be classified by their function, or bathroom products can be sorted into solids, liquids and gases.

Identifying and classifying is often connected to other types of enquiries. These include **fair testing** to compare the properties and behaviour of different materials; **pattern seeking** to find a correlation between different characteristics; **research** using secondary sources to find out more information than can be gained from observation; or finding out about how established classification criteria can be used to identify things and put them into groups.

Starting points for Indentifying and Classifying

LIVING THINGS

Alive or not alive

How can we identify what's alive and not alive? Are there things where it is difficult to tell?

Minibeasts

We found lots of minibeasts around the school but we don't know what they are. How can we create a key to help us identify them? How can we use the way they move to group them?

Are all worms the same? What about other minibeasts?

Other animals

How can we make a chart to show what different animals eat?

How will we decide what goes where in our collage of different animals and where they live?

How many different ways can we make keys and charts to help us identify animals?

We think that there are animals all around us. What lives in our tall trees? Does anything live in the long grass? What lives in the hedge? What lives in our pond? What lives in soil? What might live in windfall apples?

Plants

We took lots of pictures of plants on our walk. How can we identify them?

All the plants in the garden centre are muddled up. How can we sort them out?

All the seeds have fallen out of their packets. How can we sort them?

We want to make some fruit drinks using citrus fruits. How many different types are there? How do we know which is which?

Mrs Green has opened a fruit and vegetable shop but is confused by all the produce. What is the best way to organise all the fruits and vegetables?

We've collected lots of fallen leaves. How can we sort them out?

Microorganisms

What kinds of microorganisms are useful to us? How can we make a guide to them?

Ourselves

Can we identify everyone in our class by their fingerprints? What other ways can we use to identify children in the class?

Mrs Feedem wants to reorganise the food in her corner shop. Can we give her some different ideas for how to do it?

There's a school camping trip and the teachers want to make sure the meals are healthy and interesting. Can we sort food into a chart to help us decide what's best to take?

MATERIALS AND THEIR USES

Fabrics

Children have been playing with clothes in the play corner and left them all muddled up. How can we sort them out?

Which clothes will keep us cool / warm / dry on our trip?

We want to make an umbrella. There are lots of different materials we can use to make it. How can we sort the materials to find those we think will work and those that won't?

Other materials

We've got a big pile of different materials that we can recycle. How are we going to sort them for recycling?

We must have at least 14 different types of glues in the stock cupboard! They all seem to do slightly different jobs. Can we find a useful way to sort them out?

We have lots of different items to send through the post. How can we sort the packaging so we know which is best for wrapping the different items?

The pens and pencils are muddled up. How can we sort them out? Do they all write on the same surfaces?

FORCES, ENERGY AND MOVEMENT

Toys

Look, all the toys have been put in the wrong places. How can we sort them out? (e.g. by the way they move)

Can we sort our moving toys by how they are powered?

Falling

Shanaz has brought in a lovely collection of gliders, sycamore seeds, conkers, balloons, and other things. Can we help her to sort them out? (e.g. into ones that float, fall and fly)

Pushes and pulls

We've been on a push / pull walk round the school and taken photos of things we push or pull. How can we sort all the pushes and pulls we noticed on our walk round school?

Electricity and magnetism

We want to put a switch in our circuit. Which things make good switches and which don't? How can we sort them out?

We're making a magnetic game. How can we sort out things that are magnetic and those that aren't?

EARTH AND SPACE

Stars and planets

We're going to do some night sky watching. Can we make a key to help us identify which planet is which? Can we do the same for the planets' satellites?

How can we tell which constellation is which in the sky?

Rocks and soil

We've been invited to the geology museum to help them with some new rocks. How can we identify and sort all the different rock samples?

Everyone has brought in a sample of soil from where they have been on holiday. How can we identify and sort them?

SOUND

Types of sounds

We've been on a sound walk. How can we sort out the different sounds that we heard?

When the orchestra came into school, their different instruments made different sounds. Can we sort the school instruments by the sounds they make?

LIGHT

Reflection

The nights are getting darker. Can we sort our clothes to help us decide which are good to wear outside in the dark? Which materials reflect light?

Shadows

We've been making shadows and noticed that different things make different kinds of shadows. How can we sort things by the kind of shadows that they make?

What can children do when they identify and classify?

Ideas for activities

There are many different contexts in which children can carry out identifying and classifying enquiries. Some suggestions for these are given in the Starting Points table on the previous two pages, and in each of the four activities described in detail later.

Developing scientific skills and understanding

Children are surrounded by things that have been classified and organised. Trays for different equipment and resources at school, different foods in the local shops and different bins for recycled materials all illustrate how classification works. Finding out what things are, and organising them into groups, provide good contexts for children to develop the skills of identifying and classifying and a purpose for observing characteristics, similarities and differences. These skills provide a distinctive way for children to develop their understanding of scientific ideas. As children develop their skills, the depth and range of their understanding should also increase.

As in all types of science enquiry, when identifying and classifying children should become progressively more systematic and show more independence in the way they plan and carry out their enquiries. Their descriptions of objects should become more accurate and precise, moving from simple to detailed, and considering more than one potentially testable property or characteristic. Children should become increasingly sophisticated in the way they identify and classify, using more complex methods or equipment, and reference works such as field study guides. Their evaluation of their enquiries should also show an increased awareness of the effectiveness of their working methods.

Young children identify and classify objects in a very concrete way, physically matching and grouping together visually similar objects, or textures, smells, tastes and sounds. They sort different objects into different boxes and then hoops, so that they can show intersecting sets. They record how they have grouped objects using simple pictures, tables, collages, displays and photographs.

As they progress they record their classifying activities in tables, booklets, charts and guides, moving from pictorial headings to names and using increasingly scientific terminology. They use Carroll and Venn diagrams and keys for more sophisticated sorting and recording.

The grid on page 52 shows the progression of skills that children use when identifying and classifying. You can use the grid to ensure that there is sufficient challenge in the identifying and classifying enquiries that you plan.

Encouraging talk and questioning

From a very early age children notice similarities and differences, as they explore the world around them, and these lead naturally to further questions.

 Look – this one is floating! I wonder if this one does too?

Children will be fascinated by the differences between the things that interest them. You can ask questions that help children to be more precise and systematic in what they notice.

 Can you find one the same? Is this one bigger or smaller? How much heavier is it?

You might want to narrow the focus of children's observations so that they sort by identifying one feature.

 There's a box of toys in the nursery. It's in a mess. Pia wants to sort them into groups of toys that move in the same way. Talk about how you can help her.

You can indicate the sort of skills or equipment they could use.

 How can we find out which rock is which? Do we need to use a key? Or a magnifying glass? Or find out which ones are porous?

By talking about the differences and similarities they notice, children can be encouraged to turn their initial observations and wonderings into questions that can be investigated practically. With your support, they can make decisions about how to categorise objects and record their findings.

What are the possible outcomes?

Identifying and classifying enquiries will lead to different kinds of outcomes that will provide rich assessment evidence:

> physical groupings of objects

> completed tables, Venn and Carroll diagrams

> keys that children have used to identify things or that they have designed

> children thinking, talking and writing about the skills they have used

> the development of scientific understanding about diversity and variety, and the importance of classification systems in science.

Identifying and Classifying: Skills Progression Grid

	Plan	**Do**	**Review**
Foundation	• I am curious about similarities and differences • With help I ask questions about similarities and differences • I talk about my ideas for sorting or matching things	• I use my senses to sort and match things • I match things that are the same • I find things that are similar or different • I sort or group things in my own way • I use simple equipment to help me sort things (e.g. boxes, hoops)	• I talk about how I sorted or matched things
Early primary	• I ask questions about how and why things are similar or different • I decide what to observe to identify or sort things	• I make comparisons between simple features of objects, materials or living things • I record my observations in words or pictures or simple tables • I sort objects by observable and behavioural features • I record my sorting in sorting circles or tables	• I identify similarities and differences and talk about them • I begin to use simple scientific language to talk about how things are similar or different • I try to use my records to help sort or identify other things
Middle primary	• I talk about what criteria I will use to sort and classify things • I decide what equipment to use to identify and classify things • I talk about things that can be grouped and decide when questions can be answered by sorting and classifying	• I carry out simple tests to sort and classify according to properties or behaviour • I use Carroll diagrams, Venn diagrams and more complex tables to sort things • I use simple keys and branching databases to identify things • I make simple branching databases (keys) for things that have clear differences	• I draw simple conclusions about the things I have sorted and classified • I talk about the similarities and differences I identified using some scientific language • I suggest improvements to the way I sort and identify things
Late primary	• I recognise when identifying and classifying will be helpful to answer my questions • I decide what equipment, tests and secondary sources of information to use to identify and classify things	• I use a series of tests to sort and classify materials • I use secondary sources to identify and classify things • I make my own keys and branching databases with 4 or more items • I use more than one piece of scientific evidence to identify and classify things	• I draw valid conclusions when sorting and classifying • I recognise the significance of sorting and classifying • I talk about and explain what I have done using scientific knowledge • I evaluate how well my keys worked

SORTING TOYS

Children will have their own favourite toys, and they will be used to playing with them. Toys provide young children with rich opportunities to explore using their eyes, ears and sense of touch. With your encouragement they can begin to identify and match colours, textures, sounds and shapes.

It's helpful to provide access to a wide range of toys. Try to find toys with interesting features, such as the sound they make, their texture (e.g. soft toys, bouncy toys) or ways of moving, that will get children interested and talking. Give the children plenty of time at the start to play with and explore the toys, looking at materials, colours, sounds, how the toys work, textures and sizes, and to think and talk about what they notice.

Health and Safety Notes
- *Ensure that all toys are safe for children to use. Young children have a habit of putting things in their mouths.*
- *Avoid toys that are damaged or contain small parts that could be swallowed.*

Getting started

You can build on children's spontaneous observations and questions

Encourage children to talk about the toys that they play with.

These toys make a big noise.

The truck has got wheels.

You can ask questions to focus their observations

Use questions that help the children to make comparisons between toys.

Do all the toys make a noise? Do they all make the same noise? Let's sort them. Can we find other things that make the same kind of noise?

Have all the toys got wheels? Can we sort them into the toys with wheels and the toys that don't have wheels? Do they all move in the same way?

You can provide your own starting points

You can make an observation.

All the toys in the play area are in a big muddle. I wonder how we can sort them out? Can you help?

Have you seen what's on the wonder table today? Why don't you go and play with them? I've put some boxes by the table. Can you sort the things out into different boxes?

You can make links with how children use toys at home.

You can all bring a toy in to school tomorrow. I wonder how many different kinds of toys we will have?

When the shopkeeper went home all the toys in the toyshop sneaked off their shelves and played and ran around. In the morning she opened the door and they were in a huge muddle. Can you help the shopkeeper to sort them out and get them back on the shelves in the right places?

WHAT CAN CHILDREN DO?

IDEAS FOR ACTIVITIES

Children can:

> play 'I spy' or 'guess what I am' games, with clues, to begin to identify features of toys

> play 'feely bag' games where they have to describe a toy without naming it

> focus on particular types of toys (e.g. a focus on moving toys would help to develop their early ideas about force and movement, or a focus on what the toys are made of would help to develop early ideas about materials)

> sort toys into boxes, baskets, hoops and bags

> use hoops to begin to think about overlapping groups

> create a tidy toy shop by organising toys that you have muddled up when the children are not present. They might do this in the context of a story (e.g. untidy shopkeeper)

> use pictures from catalogues to sort toys into groups and make posters of them

> play matching games with toys, or pictures of toys. (e.g. I have a teddy here. Who has a toy that they think is something like the teddy? Ben's chosen a duck because it's yellow like the teddy. That's a good idea. Does anyone else have a yellow toy?)

> play 'find a friend' where they choose a toy and see how many toys, held by other children, they can link to their toy.

DEVELOPING SKILLS AND UNDERSTANDING

Give children lots of opportunities to:

> talk to each other about how they might sort the toys, the choices they are making, what the toys are and how the toys work

> describe the colours, textures, movement or sounds, and talk about the senses they will use to do this

> ask questions about the toys as they explore and sort

> look, listen and feel carefully to group the toys

> find examples of toys that have similar features

> compare how they sorted the toys with what other children have done

> develop and use key vocabulary (e.g. push, pull, move, roll, bounce, clockwork, wind up, battery, different, same as, hard, soft).

Encouraging talk and questioning

Try to help children to raise their own questions by giving them time to talk together and share what they already know about toys. A period of initial play and exploration will help them to do this. You can help them to turn the ideas that they share into questions to explore.

Patrick and Sharmila said they had lots of toys with wheels. Do all the toys with wheels work in the same way?

Lots of you said all the toys were different. I wonder if there is anything the same about some of them. Can you think of anything?

Ask questions to encourage them to talk together about how they might put toys in groups and chat together about what they are doing. This may need some adult support, but give them time to work on their own before intervening.

I wonder if we could sort them into the ways that they work? What's the same about them? What's different about them?

Did anyone think about how the toys feel? Can you tell what they are without looking? I wonder if we could sort them by how they feel?

Encourage children to talk about how they have sorted the toys. They may need to work in small groups to do this.

You have all sorted different toys. Let's tell each other what we did. Did we put the same toys in different groups?

You can help them to raise more questions to investigate in different ways by being puzzled by something that they found out.

I'm puzzled about something. When Poppy and Gino helped to tidy the play area they put all the dolls together. I wondered if all the dolls are the same? Are they made of the same material? Do they look the same? Do they feel the same?

What are the possible outcomes?

Encouraging children to explore, match and sort toys leads to different kinds of outcomes

These can provide rich assessment evidence of their developing skills and understanding.

For example:

> what they say to each other, and you, about how they explored the toys, what they found out, and how they decided to sort them

> their descriptions of similarities and differences in colour, texture, movement, sound, etc. (e.g. both these toys are bouncy; if you push these this one will roll but the other one won't)

> how they identify different toys and describe the different features

> the ways that they sorted toys and the range of different ways of sorting that they used

> physical records they made of the sorted toys

> pictures of sorted toys made from magazine pictures

> photographs of groups of toys, or of the toys in the play area, to show how they sorted their toys

> what they say about toys and the ways that toys work (e.g. clockwork, battery, push, pull).

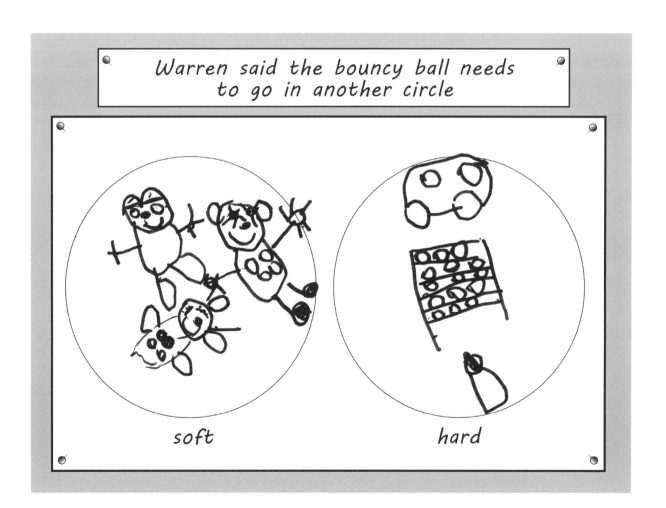

Warren said the bouncy ball needs to go in another circle

soft   hard

Questions that can lead to other types of enquiry

Questions that children may ask (or you could ask them)

All these toys have got wheels, I wonder which one will roll the furthest?

All these toys make a noise. Which one is the loudest?

This toy hasn't got batteries. Why does it make a noise?

I want to find the bounciest ball in the toy box. How can I find out which it is?

Which truck is fastest? How can I work it out?

How can you add challenge?

Children can be encouraged to:

> suggest new ways of sorting the toys

> recognise that some of their sorting criteria are opposites (e.g. rough and smooth)

> make a drawing of some of their groupings

> identify things that belong in overlapping groups

> look for different types of one toy (e.g. dolls) that they can sort in different ways.

SORTING FRUITS AND VEGETABLES

Fruits and vegetables are a rich context for identifying and classifying. They come in a myriad of shapes, sizes, colours and textures, and most of them are easy for children to handle. Children will be familiar with common fruits and vegetables, such as apples and carrots, and supermarkets tend to stock a wide range of less familiar examples.

Encourage children to use all their senses to explore fruits and vegetables before they begin to think about how they might sort and classify them. This activity will help children to learn about plants, parts of plants and how they grow. They will also begin to understand the roles of fruits and vegetables in plant growth and seed dispersal.

Health and Safety Notes

- *Fruits and vegetables are normally safe to eat, though some individuals may have allergies. Make yourself aware of these and take appropriate action.*
- *The fruits and vegetables can be tasted provided that all the usual food hygiene precautions are taken, including cleaning the food, washing hands and keeping surfaces clean. If this is not possible, discuss with the children why eating the fruits and vegetables is not appropriate in this instance.*

Getting started

You can build on children's spontaneous observations and questions

Many schools have fruit snack time that can offer good opportunities for talking about and tasting fruits and vegetables.

I like red fruits best. Carrots are very crunchy. If I have strawberries in my lunch box they get squashed. I don't like lemons.

You can ask questions to focus their observations

Use questions that help the children to make comparisons between fruits and vegetables.

Does anyone like green fruits? Can anyone think of something else that's crunchy? Does anything else squash easily?

Has anybody been to the vegetable stall on the market? How do customers find what they want? How does the person in charge organise all the different things for sale?

Look, I've got a purple carrot! Which of your groups will you put it in?

You can provide your own starting points

You could use stories as starting points.

The greengrocer has got in a big muddle with all the different vegetables! How can we help her to sort them out?

I've got a basket of fruits and vegetables. Draw me a picture of what you think we will find inside them. Could that help us to sort them?

Let's go and visit the supermarket to find out how they organise the fruits and vegetables. What will we look for? What questions shall we ask?

WHAT CAN CHILDREN DO?

IDEAS FOR ACTIVITIES

Children can:

> look closely using hand lenses and digital microscopes and take pictures to help identify key parts of fruits and vegetables

> focus on particular types of fruits and vegetables (e.g. vegetables that grow underground)

> play a 'yes/no/maybe so' game to help identify features of fruits and vegetables (e.g fruits have seeds inside, a carrot has a bushy top)

> sort fruits and vegetables into shopping bags, hoops, trays, etc.

> use hoops to identify which belong in overlapping groups

> decide ways of organising fruits and vegetables that are muddled up. They might do this in the context of a story (e.g. untidy shopkeeper)

> create a collage or poster of grouped fruits and vegetables using photographs or pictures from catalogues

> play matching games with fruits and vegetables (e.g. who has a fruit that they think is something like the tomato? Khalida has chosen an apple because it's got a smooth skin like the tomato. Does anyone else have one with a smooth skin?)

> play 'find a friend' where they choose a fruit or vegetable and see how many fruits or vegetables held by other children they can link to theirs

> use what they have learnt to help them write a mini guide to fruits and vegetables.

DEVELOPING SKILLS AND UNDERSTANDING

Give children lots of opportunities to:

> talk to each other about the fruits and vegetables, how they might sort them, and what the similarities and differences are between them

> talk together about what they've done, and compare their sorting criteria with others

> ask questions about the things they find out about fruits and vegetables as they explore

> suggest different ways of sorting (observable and non-observable)

> record their sorting in drawings, photographs, or tables

> develop and use key vocabulary (e.g. fruit, vegetable, seed, leaf, stem, root, grow, plant, different from, similar to).

Encouraging talk and questioning

Encourage the children to look carefully at a selection of real fruits and vegetables (rather than plastic ones or photographs) or plan a visit to a greengrocer or supermarket. Encourage them to talk about their ideas. The initial exploration will help them to do this.

Talk to each other about what you noticed when you were exploring the fruits and vegetables.

You said that they were different shapes. What different shapes are there? How can we sort them? Can we put the long thin ones in one group and all the round ones in another?

You can extend their ideas by encouraging children to think and talk about observable (e.g. shape, colour, taste, smell, stackability, squashability, heaviness, perishability) and non-observable features (e.g. part of plant, where grown, how to prepare or cook, when in season, how many of the children like the taste) of the fruits and vegetables.

Has anybody eaten these at home? Did you cook them first?

The squashed raspberries have left a stain. Does anything else leave a stain?

This one's gone mouldy. We don't want to eat that! Do you think any of the others might go mouldy?

Encourage children to talk about what they have found out.

Talk to another group about how you sorted the fruits and vegetables. Did you have the same ideas? Were there any things you did not recognise?

You can help them to raise more questions to investigate in different ways by being puzzled by something that they found out.

One group said that the strawberry was the only fruit that has seeds on the outside. I wonder if that's right? How we could find out?

Chat with your partner to share ideas about what you are puzzled about. We can put them in our 'Puzzle book' and see if between us we can find out the answers.

What are the possible outcomes?

Exploring, matching and sorting fruits and vegetables leads to different kinds of outcomes

These can provide rich assessment evidence of their developing skills and understanding.

For example:

> what they say to each other, and you, about how they identified the fruits and vegetables and how they decided to sort them

> the different ways they use to sort fruits and vegetables

> drawings or photographs of the ways that they have grouped fruits and vegetables

> their descriptions and records of similarities and differences

> their written and oral responses when they play the 'yes/no/maybe so', matching and 'find a friend' games

> how they use aids such as hand lenses and digital microscopes to look closely at the fruits and vegetables

> detailed drawings and photographs of fruits and vegetables and any annotations that they include

> the posters or collages that they make

> the content of their mini guides.

Thea said that fruits and vegetables roll in different ways because of their shape

Questions that can lead to other types of enquiry

How do they get squishy fruits to the shops without them getting squashed?

I wonder how long it takes for a carrot to grow?

Can anyone grow their own fruits and vegetables? How would you grow them if you didn't have a farm or a big garden?

What time of year do they grow?

Does the same fruit always have the same number of seeds?

What's the world record for the biggest pumpkin? I wonder if we can grow one just as big?

How can you add challenge?

Children can be encouraged to:

› use comparisons rather than straightforward yes or no answers to classify fruits and vegetables (e.g. this is more juicy, this one is the heaviest)

› use secondary sources to find out more about the similarities and differences, and how and where different fruits and vegetables grow

› compare fruits and vegetables that grow locally and those grown in other countries, and begin to think about the implications of transporting them.

MINIBEAST GUIDES AND KEYS

Minibeasts are fascinating! They come in lots of different shapes and sizes and offer rich opportunities for identification and classification. Children are likely to be familiar with a small range of minibeasts, such as worms and spiders, but there will be lots that they have not come across. Many minibeasts hibernate or spend the winter as eggs or pupae, so the best time of year to do this activity is when the weather is warm.

Children can use ready-made keys and spotter guides, and go on to make their own simple classification key or guide. Creating keys is more demanding than making spotter guides. It is helpful to give children an opportunity to use different guides and keys to understand how these work. These are readily available in books and on the internet, as well as through specialist organisations such as the Field Studies Council. This activity will help children to learn more about the rich diversity of animals and how they survive, and should work with any selection of flora and fauna.

Health and Safety Notes

- Follow the school's guidelines for working out of doors. Check that areas are safe for children to visit. Take particular care near ponds.
- Some children may have allergies. Take appropriate action. Avoid handling hairy caterpillars. Ensure that children wash their hands after handling minibeasts or soil and that any cuts are covered.
- See ASE Be Safe! page 13.

Getting started

You can build on children's spontaneous observations and questions

Encourage children to be aware of animals in their environment so that they begin to notice them in their everyday lives.

> There are a lot of insects on the plant by the gate. We think that they are greenfly but we're not sure.
>
> We found this on the bushes. Is it a centipede?

You can ask questions to focus their observations

Ideally children need to encounter creatures with different observable features e.g. spiders, snails, slugs, beetles, centipedes, worms, ants and caterpillars.

> Look carefully. What colours are they? Do they have wings? How many legs do they have? What else can you see?
>
> How would we find out what kind they are? Have you ever seen a key for identifying animals?

You can provide your own starting points

You could get started by organising a tree shake, or a pond dip, or a hunt through some leaf litter.

> We're going to visit a country park tomorrow. What kind of minibeasts do you think we will see? We're going to make a minibeast guide for the school when we get back. What kinds of things will we need to look for?
>
> We're going to have a minibeast quiz, and you can decide on the questions. It's about minibeasts around the school. Let's go outside to find out more.

> You can get different spotter guides for minibeasts. The headteacher wants to know which we should buy. Let's try them out and see which we think is best.
>
> The younger children need some help to identify minibeasts. Can you make a guide to minibeasts for them to use?

Children will need plenty of opportunity to observe and talk about the creatures they find before they identify them and start to create a key of their own.

WHAT CAN CHILDREN DO?

IDEAS FOR ACTIVITIES

Children can:

> locate minibeasts by shaking them out of bushes onto a white sheet, or looking under stones, or looking under leaf litter or logs

> observe minibeasts in their habitats and make detailed records of what they observe, including making sketches and taking photographs

> with care, bring limited numbers of minibeasts into the classroom to observe more closely (they must be returned to where they were found as soon as possible)

> look at minibeasts using a digital camera and take photographs or short film sequences of them

> use spotter guides to identify what they have found, think about how spotter guides work and create their own

> use keys to identify what they have found, think about how keys work and create their own

> compare keys and other information sources

> play a 'what am I?' game, where the names of the minibeasts are put on sticky labels on their backs or on hats where they can't see them. They have to guess what they are by asking questions

> think and talk about the skills that they used to create their keys and guides.

DEVELOPING SKILLS AND UNDERSTANDING

Give children lots of opportunities to:

> talk to each other about the features of minibeasts, what the similarities and differences are between them, and how they might identify and sort them

> raise questions about minibeasts based on their observations

> describe the minibeasts using different observable features

> record using photographs, drawings, guides and keys

> talk with each other about what they've done, evaluate their own keys and compare their keys and guides with others

> develop and use key vocabulary (e.g. structure, body parts, antennae, wings, legs, thorax, abdomen, eyes, identification, classify, key, different from, similar to).

Encouraging talk and questioning

Children will talk readily about the animals that they are observing. Encourage the children to talk about observable features (e.g. colour, shape of body, number of legs, ways of moving) as well as where they might be found. You can ask questions to help focus their conversation.

What can you see when you look at the minibeasts?

Can you see a pattern in how they move their legs?

Can you see a mouth? What do you think they might eat?

How will you record your ideas?

Encourage them to do their own research to help them to identify what they have found, by talking to each other and using information sources. You can also encourage talk and careful observation by getting them to ask each other questions about the minibeasts.

How many different types do you think you have? Can you think of how we might sort them into groups?

What features shall we look for to identify the different minibeasts? Work in your trios to decide. Let's see how many different ideas we have.

What other things can we find out about the minibeasts that might help us to make our own guide?

They can try using each other's guides or keys. Encourage them to think of questions to ask each other.

Have a look at the guide that this group made. Think about the minibeasts that you looked at. How well will the guide work? What questions do you want to ask them about their guide?

What other ways could we sort them? How can we record what we do?

When they have finished, encourage them to talk about and evaluate the process of making the guides or keys.

Pair up with another group. Talk about which sources of information were the most useful. What was it about them that helped?

What have you learnt by looking at each other's guides? Do you want to make any changes to your own guide?

What are the possible outcomes?

Identifying and classifying minibeasts leads to different kinds of outcomes

These can provide rich assessment evidence of their developing skills and understanding.

For example:

> - what they say to each other, and you, about how they identified and sorted the minibeasts

> - drawings and photographs that they make of minibeasts and annotations they include

> - the way they talk about the content of photographs and drawings

> - their descriptions of similarities and differences between minibeasts

> - how they play the 'what am I?' game

> - how they use guides and keys and what they say and write about how they are used to identify animals

> - how they use information sources to support their learning

> - how they create their own guides or keys

> - the content of their own guides or keys to minibeasts

> - their evaluation of the guides or keys that they made.

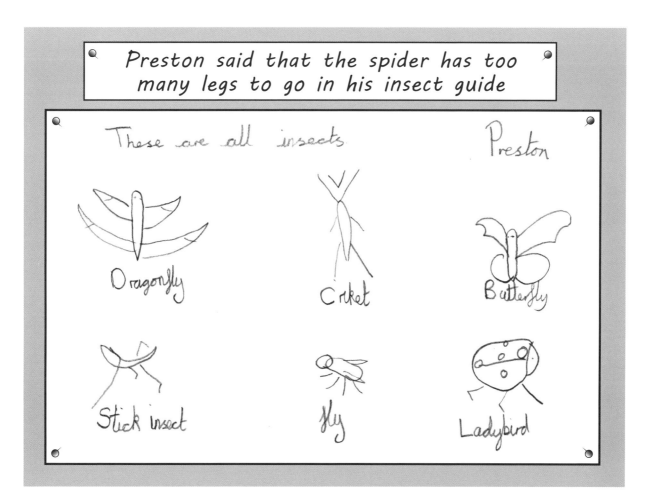

Questions that can lead to other types of enquiry

My favourite minibeast is a woodlouse, how can I find out more about it?

I want to find a spider but don't know where to look. Where can I learn about where it lives to help me find one?

I think that worms eat soil but I'm not sure. I wonder if there is a way of checking my ideas?

Lots of animals eat minibeasts. I don't want my minibeast to get eaten so I need to find out what might eat it and how it can keep safe.

I wonder if my minibeast is sleepy in the mornings and wide awake after lunch just like me?

How can you add challenge?

Children can be encouraged to:

> ask questions that require more detailed observation

> compare their guides with published ones

> try out their guides and keys with groups of younger children

> develop criteria for evaluating guides and keys that other children make

> develop guides or keys for other animals or plants, including creating a key that has more than two choices (e.g no legs, two pairs of legs, three pairs of legs, more than three pairs of legs)

> evaluate which are the most useful questions for sorting minibeasts when making a key.

GROUPING BATHROOM PRODUCTS

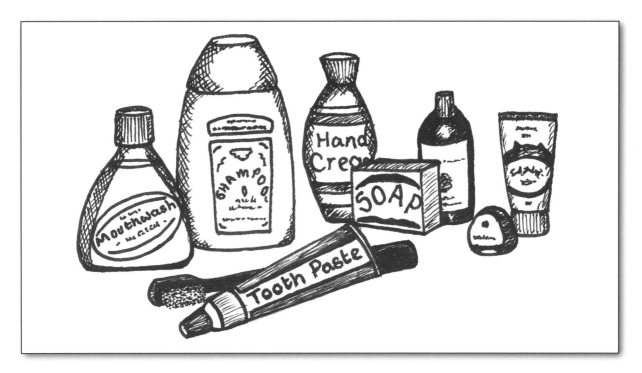

A visit to the bargain basket in a chemists shop, or scouring the shelves of a discount store, will result in a fascinating opportunity to explore, sort and classify solids, liquids and gases in the form of bathroom products. Bathroom products do not always sit neatly into one of the three categories. For example, some gels can be runny when stirred, but set and become more solid when exposed to the air, and sit somewhere between solid and liquid. Talcum powder moves like a liquid but is actually very tiny bits of solid.

Children can use criteria other than solids, liquids and gases to sort the products in order to develop their skills of identifying and classifying. This activity provides older children with a more challenging opportunity to identify and classify, and learn that the world is not always organised into neat groups. Exploring the substances inside and out of their containers can be useful as a starting point.

Health and Safety Notes

- *All products should be checked for safety warnings. Children should be told not to put any of the substances into their mouths and to wash their hands if they get any of the products on them. Do not use bathroom cleaning or disinfecting products or anything containing bleach. Take care with aerosols.*
- *Do not use prescription medicines and take care with other medical products such as indigestion tablets. Supervise their use as appropriate.*

Getting started

You can build on children's spontaneous observations and questions

Gather together a wide variety of different bathroom products (bars of soap, liquid soap, shower gel, shampoo, conditioner, hair gel, talc, toothpaste, mouth wash, shaving foam, body lotion, etc.) and encourage the children to explore the labels and contents of the bottles and jars.

Encourage children to begin to look for things that are in different states in their everyday lives.

> *Is hair gel liquid or solid? I think it's solid because it doesn't pour.*
>
> *What is talcum powder? What's it for?*

You can ask questions to focus their observations

Use questions that help children make comparisons.

> *Are there other things like hair gel? Let's have a look at them. How can we decide where to put them if we are sorting solids and liquids?*
>
> *How could we find out more about talcum powder? Shall we have a closer look at it? Let's get the digital microscope out.*

You can provide your own starting points

You can share observations that you have made.

> *I went to the shop to buy some things for the bathroom and when I got home I started thinking about what they were. I was very puzzled about some of them. I didn't know whether they were solids, liquids or gases. I couldn't work out which was which. Can you help me?*

> *This gel is runny in the pot, but when my son puts it on his hair it goes hard. Is it a liquid or not? Are there other things like that?*
>
> *The shaving foam sounds like a liquid if you shake it, but when it comes out it isn't runny! What's going on?*

WHAT CAN CHILDREN DO?

IDEAS FOR ACTIVITIES

Children can:

> explore the products and create lists of characteristics that they could use to sort them

> create groupings of the products and record them using drawings or photographs

> talk about and research properties of solids, liquids and gases, and use this to sort the bathroom products, then try to create a sequence from solid to gas. Where would each product go?

> add other products to their groupings

> create a shop shelf in the classroom, organising the products in interesting ways

> make a mini guide to bathroom products or a key for sorting them

> play a 'what am I?' game where the names of the products are put on sticky labels on their backs or on hats where they can't see them. They have to guess what they are by asking questions

> play a 'find a friend' game where every child is wearing a hat or label with a product on it. Each child carries a card. They write down the name of any other product they can connect to and why. Compare lists. Which products have the longest lists and why?

DEVELOPING SKILLS AND UNDERSTANDING

Give children lots of opportunities to:

> talk with each other about the products, their different properties and states of matter, and decide on ways of sorting them

> raise questions based on what they observe

> sort the products according to their characteristics and record their findings in tables and graphs

> use secondary sources of information (e.g. product labels)

> talk together about what they've done and compare how they used their sorting criteria

> create sorting keys

> develop and use key vocabulary (e.g. solid, liquid, gas, mixture, texture, consistency, flow, volume, properties, evaporate).

Encouraging talk and questioning

You can encourage children to explore and talk together about bathroom products. It is helpful to ask questions that begin to focus their observations.

I want you to have a really good look at these bathroom products. I've got some questions to get you started and then it's over to you!

How do you get it out of its container?

What is it used for?

How can you describe its texture?

Does it always look and feel the same?

Encourage them to think and talk about how they might sort them by observable characteristics.

Work with a partner to think about how to sort them. What will you look for? What are the important features?

How do you think we could classify them? Do some fit into more than one group?

After they have sorted their products encourage them to evaluate the process and think of more questions to investigate.

Work with another pair to share what you did. How did you decide which fits into each group?

Were there any that you do not agree about? Write them down and we can share them with the rest of the class. How can we sort out our disagreements? Will we do some research or is a practical enquiry better?

What other ways could we sort them? How can we record what we do?

What are the possible outcomes?

Grouping bathroom products leads to different kinds of outcomes

These can provide rich assessment evidence of their developing skills and understanding.

For example:

- › what they say to each other, and you, about how they decided to sort the products
- › their recordings of how they grouped the products
- › the way that they sequence the products from solids to gases
- › the way they the organise the products on a 'shop shelf' in the classroom
- › their written and oral descriptions of similarities and differences between the products and why they belong to certain groups
- › the language that they use when they talk about the products
- › their responses to the 'what am I' and 'find a friend' games
- › how they use information sources to support their learning
- › the content of their mini guides
- › their evaluation of the way that they grouped the products.

> ## Maddy said that some things could be put into more than one group

Solids — Liquids — Gases

Solids: bath bomb, soap, bath salts

Liquids: mouthwash, body-wash, conditioner, shampoo, tooth-paste, body-wash, roll-on deodrant, nail-polish remover, perfume, hair putty, face scrub

Gases: spray-on deodrant, hair spray, body spray, shaving foam

maddy

Questions that can lead to other types of enquiry

Questions that children may ask (or you could ask them)

Where do bathroom products come from?

What happens if you leave the container open?

Is runny hair gel easier to use? Which brand is the runniest?

These indigestion tablets say that they neutralise acid in the stomach. How can we find out whether that is true?

Are bathroom products dangerous? Do they affect the environment?

Which brands are the best value for money?

How can you add challenge?

Children can be encouraged to:

> be more precise in their comparison of the products and make greater use of scientific language

> find creative ways to record their investigations of the products

> recognise products that are mixtures of substances in different states (e.g. shaving foam, facial scrub)

> evaluate the suitability for intended purpose, effectiveness or value for money of different brands.

PATTERN SEEKING **I** Introduction

What is Pattern Seeking?

In pattern seeking enquiries children observe, measure and record events and systems. They also collect and interpret data from secondary sources. They make observations and conduct surveys where the variables can't easily be controlled for practical or ethical reasons. In these activities children try to answer questions by identifying patterns in the observations and measurements that they record. Sometimes they will find a direct relationship between variables. For example, they might observe that the thicker strings on a guitar produce deeper notes. In this case there is a direct cause and effect relationship between the thickness of the string and the pitch of the note. Sometimes the relationship is less obvious. It is more common to find that two things are associated together without one causing the other. For example, people with big hands tend to have big feet, or materials that are good sound insulators also tend to be good thermal insulators.

Pattern seeking enables children to find out more about people, other animals and plants in their environments, and develop an understanding of fundamental ideas in sciences like geology, astronomy and meteorology. Children learn about associations and causal relationships between phenomena in the world around them. These types of enquiries provide rich contexts for children to learn about habitats, adaptation and interdependence, diet, health and disease, microorganisms, weather and the solar system. They link readily with activities in other curriculum areas, especially design and technology, mathematics and English.

The table on the next page shows examples of starting points for pattern seeking.

Getting started

Opportunities for pattern seeking arise where children's curiosity and exploration of the world lead them to notice patterns and connections, such as some children can jump further than others, people have different colour eyes, or the daisies by the path are shorter than those near the hedge. You can help them to turn these observations into questions that they can investigate.

However not all pattern seeking activities will be initiated by children. You can also help children to notice things and look for patterns, such as some things might float or sink depending on how much air they contain.

Pattern seeking may be the first stage in other types of enquiry. As children notice patterns, they ask questions that lead to more systematic testing where they can control variables. For example, they notice that different elastic bands make different noises when they are stretched and plucked, and they set up a series of **fair tests** where they change the length and thickness of the elastic band. Pattern seeking can also lead to **grouping and classifying** on the basis of the patterns that they notice; to **observing over time** to spot chronological patterns (such as daily tides); and to **research** using secondary sources to help interpret and explain patterns.

Starting points for Pattern Seeking

Birds

The birds are coming to our bird table. Do different birds come at different times of the day? Do they prefer different food? Do birds with the same beaks eat the same kind of food?

Do they sing at different times during the day?

Minibeasts

There are lots of bees on the yellow flowers. Do different insects prefer different flowers? Is it to do with height, colour, scent or shape? Do snails move more on wet or dry ground?

Where do we find most snails / spiders / worms / woodlice? When are worms most active?

Other animals

We've been looking at pictures of animals and they look like they have different mouths and teeth. Do animals with the same diets have the same types of mouths and teeth? Is there a pattern between diet and shape of teeth?

Which food / living place do animals prefer? Do animals that look similar prefer the same things?

Fruit

We noticed that our apples have five seeds. Do all apples have the same number of seeds?

Do the biggest fruits have the most seeds?

Trees

I think the leaves on the tree outside school are changing. Is there a pattern to the way the leaves change colour in the autumn? Do different trees change at different times? What happens if they are in other parts of the country? Do taller trees, or trees with bigger leaves, lose their leaves before other trees? Are the tallest trees the oldest?

Other plants

Our beans grew faster than our tomatoes. Is there a pattern in the time it takes different plants to grow and how big they grow? Do tall plants grow bigger leaves? Do tall plants grow from bigger seeds?

Our beans seem to be growing anti-clockwise. Do all climbing plants curl in the same direction?

Which plants grow on the shady side of the field? Do plants in the shade grow bigger leaves than plants that grow in bright conditions?

Are all daisy leaves the same? Is there a pattern in where they grow?

Do all flowers have the same number of petals?

Which vegetables freeze and defrost without being damaged? Is there a pattern?

Ourselves

The biggest man in the world has the biggest feet. Is there a pattern between height and foot size? Do the tallest people have the strongest grip?

Are the oldest children in our class the tallest? Are the oldest adults the tallest? When does the pattern between height and age change?

Can the people with the biggest hands grab the most sweets?

Do children with the longest legs run fastest? Do the fastest runners in the class have the fastest resting pulse rate? Is there a pattern between exercise and pulse rate?

Microorganisms

Many children have been ill and off school. Is there a pattern in the way tummy bugs go round the school?

MATERIALS AND THEIR USES

Change of state

I think little things take longer to melt. Is there a pattern in how long it takes different sized snowmen and ice lollies to melt?

FORCES, ENERGY AND MOVEMENT

Floating and sinking

I think things weigh less in water. What happens when you weigh the same objects suspended in air and water? Is there a pattern?

Falling

The little fluffy feather floated slowly. Do all our feathers fall in the same way?

Movement

How many turns of the clockwork key are needed to make our toy car go 1 metre, 2 metres, etc? Is there a pattern?

How many winds of the elastic band make our bottle roller go 1 metre, 2 metres, etc? Is there a pattern?

Electricity and magnetism

This paper clip is magnetic and a good conductor of electricity. Are things that are magnetic always good conductors of electricity?

EARTH AND SPACE

Weather

It's windy and rainy today. Is it always windy when it's raining? Does rain last longer when it's windy? When are the wettest / windiest seasons? Is the weather the same in other countries?

The litter collects in one corner of the playground. Does the wind always blow in that direction?

Seasons

'Spring is starting earlier every year'. Is that right? Is there any evidence?

Rocks and soil

Here's a soil map for our area. Can we find any patterns in the places where different types of soil are found? Is there a pattern in the different plants that grow in them?

Earthquakes

There was an earthquake in Japan. Do some places have more earthquakes than others? Are the earthquakes stronger in some places than others?

Planets

The Earth takes about 365 days to go round the Sun. Does every planet take the same amount of time to go round the Sun? Is there a pattern between the size of the planet and the time it takes? Is there a pattern between the distance the planet is from the Sun and the time it takes?

SOUND

Instruments

The big, metal tuba makes a deep sound. What patterns do we find when we look at musical instruments?

Noise

I think it's always noisiest first thing in the morning. Is there a link between the amount of noise in school and time of day? Is there a link between the amount of noise and locations around the school?

What can children do when pattern seeking?

Ideas for activities

There are many different contexts in which children can carry out pattern seeking enquiries. Some suggestions for these are given in the Starting Points table on the previous two pages, and in each of the four activities described in detail later.

Developing scientific skills and understanding

From almost as soon as they are born, babies recognise that there are patterns in how things happen. Lights and sounds come from particular places, toys fall to the ground when thrown, and an adult (usually) arrives when you cry. Finding out more about these patterns means finding out more about the world and how it operates. As they get older, being able to test an idea or solve a problem continues to provide an incentive for children to collect data and look for patterns. Stimulating pattern seeking enquiries that capture children's attention provide particularly good contexts for them to use and develop the skills of observing, measuring, recording, presenting and interpreting data. These skills provide a distinctive way for children to develop their understanding of scientific ideas. As children develop their skills, the depth and range of their understanding should also increase.

As in all types of scientific enquiry, children should become progressively more systematic and show more independence in the way they plan and carry out their pattern seeking enquiries. Their observations and measurements should become more accurate and precise, moving from simple description to detailed observation and careful measurements. Children should learn to recognise the importance of selecting a suitable sample size in order to account for natural variation in samples. They should become increasingly sophisticated in the way they interpret their observations and use them to identify relationships and associations, drawing on more complex scientific ideas to explain their findings. Their evaluation of their enquiries should also show an increased awareness of the effectiveness of their working methods.

In pattern seeking enquiries children collect observations and measurements. These can be recorded in different formats, such as numeric, pictures, notes, tables and bar graphs. They might use digital cameras, video recorders, data loggers and web cams.

The purpose of pattern seeking is to find a relationship between two or more sets of data, so it can be useful to present results in scatter graphs, plotting dots to see whether there is a connection between two sets of data and identifying trends and anomalous results.

The grid on page 82 shows the progression of skills that children use when engaging in pattern seeking. You can use the grid to ensure that there is sufficient challenge in the pattern seeking enquiries that you plan.

Encouraging talk and questioning

There are lots of patterns that children might notice in their everyday lives. They should be encouraged to think and talk about whether there are reasons for these patterns.

> *Why are there so many butterflies on the buddleia?*

You can help children to turn their observations into questions that lead to more systematic enquiries. You can do this by reflecting their observations back to them, inviting suggestions for possible activities.

> *Is that the only place we find butterflies?*

You can pose a question or make an observation that encourages them to think about two data sets and possible reasons for patterns.

> *I read in a newspaper that left-handed people are better at throwing. Do you think it's true? How could we find out?*

By talking together about the patterns they have found, children can be encouraged to use evidence to defend or refute an opinion and think of new problems to solve.

> *We read on the internet that left-handed people are good at music. We didn't find this in our class. I wonder why we got a different answer?*

By giving children the opportunity to talk with you and each other, they can be encouraged to think about how they will use pattern seeking to find answers to their initial questions. They can share what they find out and, with your support, learn to make decisions about how to record and communicate their findings.

What are the possible outcomes?

Pattern seeking enquiries will lead to different kinds of outcomes that will provide rich assessment evidence:

> observation and survey evidence from different sets of data

> descriptions of patterns between data sets and identifying anomalous results

> the development of scientific understanding about a range of topics

> children thinking, talking and writing about the skills that they have used to collect data and identify patterns

> explanations for relationships and patterns they have observed that link their findings to their prior scientific knowledge.

Pattern Seeking: Skills Progression Grid

	Plan	Do	Review
Foundation	• I am curious about patterns • With help, I ask questions about patterns • I talk about my ideas for finding out about patterns	• I use my senses to look closely for patterns • I observe more than one thing at a time • I make simple records of what I notice (with help where necessary) • I use simple equipment to observe and record patterns	• I talk about what I have done and the patterns I noticed
Early primary	• I ask questions about why and how things are linked • With help, I decide what patterns to observe and measure and suggest how to do it	• I use non-standard units and simple equipment to record events that might be related • I record in words or pictures, or in simple prepared formats such as tables, tally charts and maps	• I identify simple patterns and talk about them • I make links between two sets of observations • I begin to use scientific language to talk about patterns • I talk about whether the pattern was what I expected
Middle primary	• I talk about where patterns might be found and decide when questions can be investigated by pattern seeking • I decide on which sets of data to collect, what observations to make and what equipment to use	• I use a range of equipment to collect data using standard measures • I make records using tables, bar charts or simple scatter graphs • I begin to use and interpret data collected through dataloggers	• I draw conclusions about simple patterns between two sets of data • I talk about patterns using some scientific language • I suggest improvements to the way I looked for patterns
Late primary	• I recognise when variables cannot be controlled and when pattern seeking will help to answer my question • I decide how detailed my data needs to be, and which equipment to use, to make my measurements as accurate as possible	• I use equipment accurately to collect observations • I record data appropriately and accurately • I present data in scatter graphs and frequency charts • I recognise patterns in results • I recognise the effect of sample size on reliability	• I draw valid conclusions from data about patterns and recognise their limitations • I recognise the significance of relationships between sets of data • I talk about and explain cause and effect patterns using scientific knowledge and understanding • I evaluate how well I looked for patterns

MINIBEAST PATTERNS

Exploratory walks around the school grounds can be a rich context for pattern seeking. The main focus should be on animals with distinctive behaviours and habitats (e.g. animals that live in dark and damp places, or bees visiting flowers) so that the patterns are easy to spot. At this stage, children are looking for simple patterns that will probably be obvious to older children and adults. Schools in urban areas usually have some areas where plants and small invertebrates can be found.

Children can be encouraged to talk and think about what they have seen and whether they find similar animals in similar places. Visiting the same areas on several occasions, and noting what they find there, will help them to see relationships. This will help them to begin to develop an understanding of pattern seeking as a process and learn about patterns in nature.

> **Health and Safety Notes**
> - *Make sure that there are no hazards in the places where you will take the children, and check that any animals or plants that you might encounter are not poisonous.*
> - *Avoid hairy caterpillars.*
> - *Follow the school's guidelines for working out of doors. Children and adults should wash their hands after handling minibeasts or looking through vegetation.*

Getting started

You can build on children's spontaneous observations and questions

If the outdoor play area has any sort of natural vegetation, it is likely that children will notice worms, woodlice, flying insects, spiders and so on. Having plenty of plants in pots or planted areas will also provide a rich source of spontaneous observations for children.

Look what I found! There are lots of wiggly things under the bucket.

Come and look! There are little things on these plants. Are they caterpillars?

You can ask questions to focus their observations

You might decide to focus children's attention on particular animals (e.g. snails, worms, ladybirds). Respond positively to observations about birds, but birds are not easy animals to use for pattern seeking because patterns can be hard to spot with animals that are so mobile.

Are there wiggly things under all the pots? Are they anywhere else?

Are there caterpillars anywhere else? Are all the caterpillars the same?

You can provide your own starting points

You could look in the school grounds, or a nearby park or wildlife area. Before you go out get children thinking and talking about what they think they might see and where.

We are going on an outdoor adventure. You are going to be detectives! We want to find out if there are special places where certain things like to live.

We will have to be very careful with anything that we find and treat it very gently.

Wiggly Worm climbed onto the leaf. 'What are you doing here?' said Curly Caterpillar, 'You don't live here.' 'Don't I?' said Wiggly, and he wiggled off on his way. Next he climbed very carefully onto a flower. 'What are you doing here?' said Busy Bee…..

WHAT CAN CHILDREN DO?

IDEAS FOR ACTIVITIES

Children can:

> go on a hunt and play detectives, and with help, record what they find and where
> find out where we would really find a hungry caterpillar
> visit the same place on several occasions to see if the same things are there, or if something has changed
> look closely at animals using hand lenses and digital microscopes, and take pictures or videos of them
> put sticky labels or pictures on a map of the area to show where things were found
> make drawings of what they found, use these to make a wall display and add information to it when things change or new things are found
> focus on particular animals (e.g. we're going on a worm hunt!)
> look in areas that have distinctive features (e.g. boggy area, shady area, on stems of particular plants, in bushes, on vegetables)
> play a 'yes/no/maybe so' game with pictures of animals to think and talk about where they might live
> create a wildlife area in the classroom play area, using plastic models or pictures of plants or animals, so that children can think about what might be where
> with help, create information boards for the outdoor area to help other people know what they might find and where.

DEVELOPING SKILLS AND UNDERSTANDING

Give children lots of opportunities to:

> ask questions about what they find
> look carefully and talk about the living creatures and plants they find, including what they look like and where they are
> make a visual record of their observations in drawings, models or photographs
> talk about what they found and whether they noticed any patterns in where living things grow or live
> develop and use key vocabulary (e.g. living things, worms, spiders, beetles, woodlice, ants, animals, plants, damp, dry, shady).

Encouraging talk and questioning

Encourage the children to think carefully about what they might find when they go on their hunt. You can ask questions to direct their observations and help them plan what to do.

Give them time to explore with a partner.

We're going to go outside to hunt for little animals. Talk together about what you think we might find. Can you think of any living things that live in special places?

What do you know about spiders? Where do you think we might look to find them? Talk to your partner about your ideas.

Encourage them to think about new questions.

I've got a new question. Should we look underneath stones to see if anything lives there?

Should we look underneath leaves to see if anything lives there?

Do you have any new questions too?

Encourage them to share what they see with each other.

When you find a living thing please tell someone else about it. Remember to tell them where you found it.

Talk to a partner about what you found. Did you all find the same things in the same places? Can you think of any reasons why?

What are the possible outcomes?

A hunt for living things will lead to different kinds of outcomes

These can provide rich assessment evidence of their developing skills and understanding.

For example:

> what they say to each other, and you, about patterns related to the living things that they find (e.g as recorded in a floorbook)

> how carefully they observe (e.g. The bees are on the flowers. That bee is bigger and fluffier than this one.)

> the connections that they begin to make between the things that they find and the places they find them (e.g. it's always damp where we find snails)

> their drawings and photographs and any annotations that are added (generally with help)

> their response to the, 'yes, no, maybe so', game

> the ideas that they contribute to information boards, classroom displays or play area

> what they tell you about the things that they have found and what they are called.

A page from Amber's group's minibeast hunt floorbook

Questions that can lead to other types of enquiry

Questions that children may ask (or you could ask them)

Do they live here all the time?

What are they called?

Can we take them into the classroom? How can we look after them?

Do they all look like this?

What do they eat?

Do they get any bigger?

How can you add challenge?

Children can be encouraged to:

> compare what they found with what they said they might find

> observe more systematically, looking in specific places and keeping a pictorial record of what they find

> with support, collect numerical data about numbers of things found and compare these (e.g. using a simple pictogram)

> look for patterns in the physical features of what they find, and compare the physical features of animals found in similar places.

DAISY PATTERNS

A survey to find flowers for daisy chains is a good context for pattern seeking. Daisies are easy to spot and lots of children will be familiar with them. They also grow readily in short grass, so most school fields will have a good supply of daisies. If there isn't a school field available, a local park will usually be a good alternative. It is helpful to have access to another area, such as a wildlife area, where there are fewer daisies growing.

Children can do simple surveys to find out where most daisies grow and begin to think about the environmental factors that might be linked with this. Make sure that you plan this activity for before the grass cutter's visit!

Health and Safety Notes

- *Follow the school's guidelines for working out of doors.*
- *Identify hazards in the area, such as poisonous plants. Take steps to ensure that you and the children avoid them.*
- *Children and adults should wash their hands after handling plants and working outside.*

Getting Started

You can build on children's spontaneous observations and questions

Early summer often brings a rush of interest in daisies, when the little white flowers appear in grassy areas.

Look at the field! There are daisies on it!

Look at my daisy. Do you like it? It's got red on its petals.

Can we make a daisy chain? I know where daisies grow.

You can ask questions to focus their observations

Some children may not know what daisies look like so it is worth having some around to help them understand which plant you are talking about.

Has anybody else spotted daisies growing? Are the daisies everywhere?

Do they grow under the big tree?

Are there any in the middle of the football pitch?

Where are there most daisies? How can we find out?

You can provide your own starting points

You could make a daisy chain in class, and suggest a competition.

Let's see who can make the longest daisy chain. We'll need lots of daisies. Does anyone know where we will find the most daisies?

I wonder if they are always in the same places?

Jasmin and Jez found a patch of daisies on the field. They were perfect. Soon they had linked them all together. There were just enough to make a daisy chain for Jez, but there were no more left for Jasmin. What should they do...?

WHAT CAN CHILDREN DO?

IDEAS FOR ACTIVITIES

Children can:

> look for daisies in a range of locations, including where the children live

> carry out a survey over a period of time to see if the patterns change

> look for patterns in how the daisies return if the grass does get cut

> make a very long daisy chain!

> create a tally chart to show the number of daises at different locations

> create a simple map of the area being surveyed and create a visual display of where daisies are found

> use what they've learned about daisy growth to think and talk about the possible connection between growth patterns and conditions (e.g. I think that the daisies grow best where it is sunniest. Daisies don't grow well on the path.)

> compile some advice for the gardener (e.g. This is what to do to help the daisies grow – or avoid having too many daisies).

DEVELOPING SKILLS AND UNDERSTANDING

Give children lots of opportunities to:

> raise questions based on their own observations of where daisies grow

> use their experiences to suggest where they think they will find most daisies

> with support, plan what evidence to collect and how they might do it (e.g. counting the daisies in a hoop)

> working with others, record their observations in a simple table, tally or bar chart

> talk with each other about what they've found out themselves or learned from other children's results

> with help, identify simple patterns in the data (e.g there were more daisies in the short grass; there weren't many daisies under the tree)

> begin to link cause and effect in their explanations (e.g the daisies can't grow so well where lots of children play because they get trodden on)

> develop and use key vocabulary (e.g. daisy, chain, grow, more, less, pattern, map, explain).

Encouraging talk and questioning

Give children time to talk together about where they have noticed daisies. Can they identify different areas?

Has anybody noticed daisies growing? Where did you spot them?

I think we will find most daisies on the path and at the edge of the field. Do you think I am right? Talk to your partner about where you think we might find them.

Encourage them to think and talk about planning what to do.

Why don't we divide into groups and go to different places to count? Talk together about ways of finding out where most daisies grow.

Could we lay a hoop on the ground and count all the daisies that are growing inside it?

What else could we do?

When they have finished, encourage them to talk about what they have found out.

Where did you find most daisies?

Talk together in your groups to see if you can find any patterns.

Did you all find the same things? Why do you think that is?

Encourage children to raise more questions.

I've thought of another question. If we pick one daisy does another one grow? If we pick lots will lots more grow?

What questions do you have?

What are the possible outcomes?

Surveying daisy growth leads to different kinds of outcomes

These can provide rich assessment evidence of their developing skills and understanding.

For example:

> what they say to you and each other about how to find out about where daisies grow

> how they work together to carry out their survey

> the notes or drawings made when carrying out the survey

> their tally chart showing the number of daises at different locations

> their map showing the number of daises at different locations

> what they say about where they found enough daisies to make a very long daisy chain

> advice they give to a gardener about where and how daisies might grow

> what they say about patterns in their observations

> what they say about the possible connection between growth patterns and conditions.

Imogen said that more daisies grew in the short grass than in the long grass

Questions that can lead to other types of enquiry

Questions that children may ask (or you could ask them)

Is there more than one type of daisy?

If you cut a daisy flower, how long will it be before another one grows?

How strong is a daisy chain? Can we have a competition to see who can make the strongest chain?

Do any other flowers look like daisies?

Can we use the digital microscope to find out more about the parts of the flowers we can't see easily?

How can you add challenge?

Children can be encouraged to:

> check each other's figures when they count the daisies and identify the advantages of working together

> present the data in a bar chart or scatter graph

> consider what environmental factors might affect the amount of daisy growth, and suggest further questions to investigate.

BODY PATTERNS

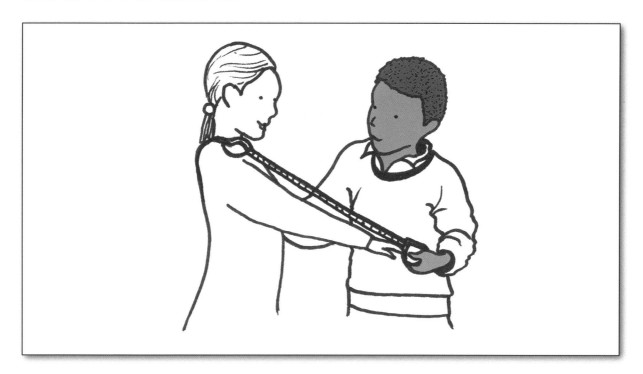

Children are fascinated by variations in size, age and physical abilities. They can readily collect data about their own bodies, such as age, height, reach, head size, hand size, hair and eye colour, speed or jumping ability. The wide range of data that they can collect provides an ideal context for pattern seeking.

As well as learning more about humans, this activity provides an opportunity for children to realise that there is not always a direct relationship between two sets of data (e.g. height and pulse rate) or that the pattern may change if you gather more data (e.g. the older you get the taller you are). You need to be sensitive to the differences between the children in your class, and avoid pattern seeking that might cause embarrassment or difficulty for some children.

Health and Safety Notes

- *Check if there are any individual health issues, such as asthma, if you plan to get the children to do any physical activity.*

Getting started

You can build on children's spontaneous observations and questions

Not all of children's observations about bodies will be usable as starting points for pattern seeking! Here are some that might be.

> *My granddad can wiggle his ears. I can't!*
>
> *Rohan must be younger than me. I'm bigger!*
>
> *These big shoes must be Laura's. She's the tallest.*
>
> *I wish my legs were longer, so I would be able to run faster.*

You can ask questions to focus their observations

This can be a good opportunity to share with children how you are using their ideas to create questions for science enquiries.

> *Can anyone else wiggle their ears?*
>
> *Are the oldest children the tallest?*
>
> *Do the tallest children have the biggest feet?*
>
> *Is it only children with long legs who run fast?*

You can provide your own starting points

The questions or problems that you use will depend on your knowledge of the children that you are working with, being sensitive to any issues that may cause them difficulties or distress.

> *We need to order new PE kit for school. Do you think that the children who need big T-shirts will need big sun hats too?*
>
> *I've just read about the tallest man in the world. I wonder how big his feet are? Do tall people always have big feet?*

> *Mrs Clark has given us this big bag of grapes. She says that we can have a handful each. Is that OK? I'll go first!*

WHAT CAN CHILDREN DO?

IDEAS FOR ACTIVITIES

Children can:

> talk to each other to identify questions to answer and data to compare
> be challenged to find interesting sets of data to compare
> work in pairs or small groups to look at different relationships in data
> look at bar charts and scatter graphs made by other children to learn what different patterns might mean
> make their own bar charts or simple scatter graphs linking two sets of data
> see if they can find any reasons for a pattern linking two sets of data where one would not be expected
> produce an 'I wonder if . . . ' wall display, where they collect questions to explore and add new patterns as they are found
> produce a class report describing the patterns they have observed or measured
> suggest solutions to problems that draw on the understanding they have developed about body size and proportionality (e.g. The people with the biggest hands will get most sweets. It would be fairer to count them and share them out equally).

DEVELOPING SKILLS AND UNDERSTANDING

Give children lots of opportunities to:

> raise questions based on differences that they have noticed
> observe and measure using lengths of string, metre rules, tape measures, etc.
> record the data in an appropriate way (e.g. tally chart, table, bar chart or scatter graph)
> identify simple patterns and trends in their observations or data
> describe what they found out and think about how cause and effect might be linked
> talk to each other to evaluate their data and how they collected it
> develop and use key vocabulary (e.g. comparison, cause, effect, scatter graph, bar chart, pattern, relationship, factors, variation).

Encouraging talk and questioning

Encourage the children to look closely at the differences between their features, relative sizes and physical abilities, and talk together about their ideas. You can ask questions to help them discuss and plan what to do to find patterns. They will need to collect two sets of data to compare and look for connections.

> Who is the tallest in the class? Who is the tallest person in the school? Are the oldest people the tallest? Will we include the teachers, or just look at the children? Talk to your partner about your ideas.
>
> Do the tallest people have the biggest feet? Can we find out by just measuring people's feet? What do you think?

Encourage the children to explore possible patterns and connections.

> If your hand is bigger can you hold more grapes? How can we find out?
>
> If someone has longer legs, will they be able to jump further? How can we find out?

After they have finished investigating you can encourage children to talk about their results.

> Work with a partner to look at what you have recorded. Can you see any patterns?
>
> Have we all found the same patterns?
>
> Can you think of a way to show the pattern that you found?

You can encourage them to raise more questions.

> I've got a question. If someone needs a bigger sweater, do they need a bigger hat too?
>
> What questions do you have? Pop your ideas on these cards so we can share them.

What are the possible outcomes?

Looking for patterns in body data leads to different kinds of outcomes

These can provide rich assessment evidence of their developing skills and understanding.

For example:

> what they say to each other, and you, about how they looked for body patterns and what they found out

> the suggestions that they make for the body patterns that they might look for

> how they use data collected by other children or adults to identify possible patterns

> how accurate their mesurements are

> their bar charts and scatter graphs and the way they write or talk about these

> their descriptions and explanations of the patterns that they have found

> the way that they analyse the patterns and unexpected patterns that they notice

> their contributions to a wall display, class book or class assembly

> the way that they evaluate what they have done.

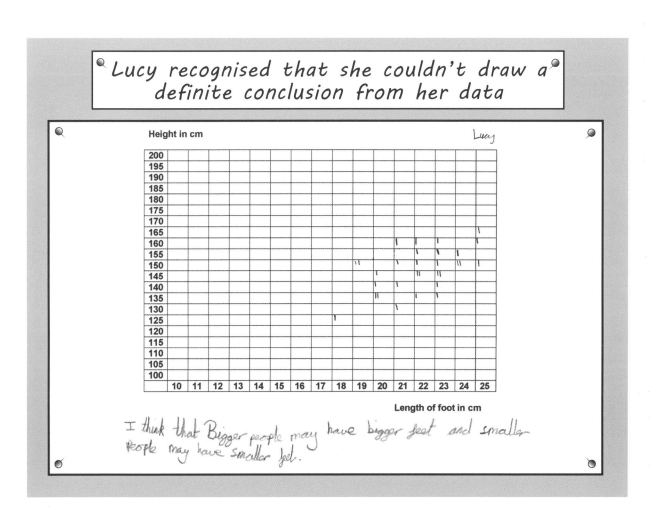

Lucy recognised that she couldn't draw a definite conclusion from her data

I think that Bigger people may have bigger feet and smaller people may have smaller feet.

Questions that can lead to other types of enquiry

Does how much I move make a difference to my pulse rate?

What makes my pulse rate go faster?

What makes my pulse rate go slower?

Who is the tallest, fastest or heaviest person in the world? Where can I find out about them?

Will I grow at the same rate every year? When will I stop growing?

I wonder if people can change what they can do by training, putting on different footwear, or using other equipment?

How can you add challenge?

Children can be encouraged to:

› choose how to present their data

› use scientific and mathematical conventions (e.g. compare hand size by area in cm²)

› begin to identify data that doesn't fit the trend and think about why this might be

› think about when the pattern between height and age changes

› identify scientific reasons for some of the patterns that they find.

WEATHER PATTERNS

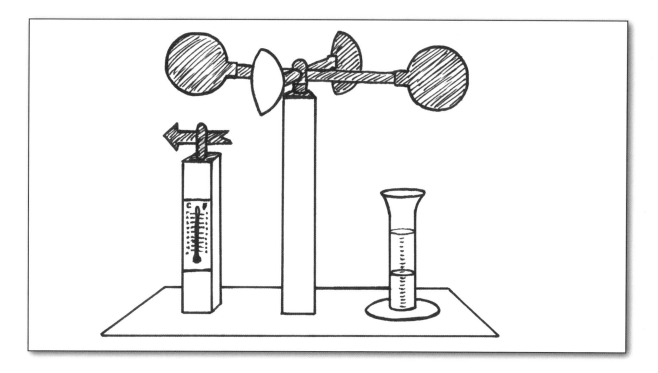

Everybody knows about the weather. It's something that we experience every day. The weather can provide fascinating questions to explore and challenging data to use for pattern seeking. Weather data is often collected in schools, but the opportunity for pattern seeking may not be exploited.

Once children start the process of thinking about possible patterns they can generate all sorts of intriguing questions. In this way they learn more about pattern seeking as a way of finding out, as well as learning more about the weather and weather patterns. Data provided by organisations such as the Met Office can be a useful source of ideas for questions, as well as supplying local and national weather data.

> ### *Health and Safety Notes*
> * *Warn children about the dangers of looking directly at the Sun.*
> * *Follow your school's guidelines for working out of doors.*
> * *Make sure that children have suitable clothing and protection when working outside in different weathers, including hats and sunscreen when appropriate.*

Getting started

You can build on children's spontaneous observations and questions

You are likely to hear comments on a regular basis about the weather. It is just a case of choosing your moment.

It always seems to be windy when it's raining.

When we collect litter it's always in the far corner of the playground. I wonder if that's the way the wind always blows?

You can ask questions to focus their observations

Try to focus your questions on possible patterns in the weather.

What data will help us decide if it's always windy when it's raining? How can we find out which way the wind usually blows in the playground?

What equipment can we use? Would using dataloggers help us? Where should we collect our data and when?

You can provide your own starting points

You can make an observation that raises a question.

Nearly every time we have a bank holiday people complain that the weather is cold and wet. Bank holidays are usually on Mondays. I wonder if Mondays really are colder and wetter? How could we find out?

Or you could use a weather saying as a starting point.

There's an old saying 'Red sky at night, shepherds' delight. Red sky in the morning, shepherds' warning'. Do you think that's true? Let's find out. What do you think we can do?

Last night on the TV news they said that it would be sunny today. It isn't! Don't the weather forecasters usually get it right?

WHAT CAN CHILDREN DO?

IDEAS FOR ACTIVITIES

Children can:

> set up a weather station and make weather monitoring equipment
> decide the best ways of gathering data
> talk together about possible patterns in the weather and connections between the weather and other phenomena (e.g. the wind direction and the way that trees grow)
> investigate possible patterns where using a datalogger could be helpful (e.g. they could use a temperature probe, and a light probe, to decide whether it's warmer at night if it has been cloudy all day)
> look at weather data on the internet or from other sources to see if they can find patterns in long term data
> compare their local data with data from other locations
> invite a weather expert into school to get access to wider data and patterns that would be difficult for them to collect just on their own
> create graphs, and charts to look for patterns
> evaluate their data and the ways that they have collected it and talk about anomalies in their data.

DEVELOPING SKILLS AND UNDERSTANDING

Give children lots of opportunities to:

> ask questions that will lead to data collection and comparison
> plan how to collect data and accurately measure it
> identify the data sets and how they will record their findings
> record the data in a chart or table, and convert the data into a graph
> identify patterns in the sets of data and talk to each other about these patterns
> use their scientific knowledge about weather to draw straightforward conclusions about cause and effect in the patterns they noticed
> evaluate how effective their investigation was and how they might improve it
> use and develop key vocabulary (e.g. pattern, anomaly, weather, sequence, rainfall, precipitation, wind strength and direction, temperature, seasonal, data).

Encouraging talk and questioning

Encourage children to explore and talk about what they know about the weather.

What special weather events can you remember? Have you noticed anything interesting about the weather recently? Work in trios to share your ideas. Make a note of your best ideas on your wipeboards.

I'm going to give you five minutes in your groups to think of anything about the weather that you have heard on the news. Let's share our ideas.

Do you think that we might find any patterns if we keep weather records? Chat to a partner about patterns we might look for.

You can encourage children to talk to each other about their ideas and the questions that they raise about possible patterns in weather data.

I've got some old weather records. What shall we look for? What questions have you got that we might be able to answer using the records?

Jenny thinks that when we have a frosty night it's clear the next day. What do you think? How can we answer that question? What could we measure and record? How long will we need to collect records?

When children have finished investigating, encourage them to talk together about what they have found.

Some groups decided that it seems to be wetter on the west side of the country than on the east side. Can anybody think of a reason why that might happen?

Talk with another group about what you found. Did you find the same patterns? Can you work out why? Can you think of any reasons why different groups might have found different patterns?

Encourage them to raise new questions.

See if you can think of new questions about the weather that we can explore. Talk about your ideas, then add your best questions to the question board.

What are the possible outcomes?

Looking for patterns in weather data leads to different kinds of outcomes

These can provide rich assessment evidence of their developing skills and understanding.

For example:

> what they say to each other, and you, about the weather and how to look for patterns

> the ideas that they have about which patterns to look for

> the ways that they gather data and talk about it

> the ways that they use the datalogger and analyse the data it provides

> the graphs and scatter graphs that they create

> how they identify and describe patterns that they have found

> the ways that they decide to record and present their data

> the ways that they use data from other sources to help them to learn

> the ideas that they share about the weather patterns either through writing or presentations

> the way that they evaluate what they have done and the ideas they offer for how to improve their pattern seeking.

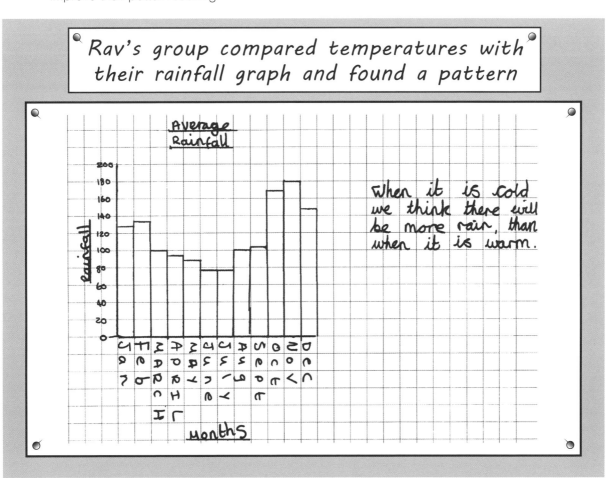

Rav's group compared temperatures with their rainfall graph and found a pattern

When it is cold we think there will be more rain, than when it is warm.

Questions that can lead to other types of enquiry

What's the difference between weather and climate?

I always feel happy when it's sunny, I wonder if weather makes a difference to how other people feel?

Can we do some tests to find out if the weather makes a difference to things like plants?

Look at the bubbles floating in the air. We wonder if we can use them to find out more about the wind?

I wonder what it would be like to be a cloud? Could we make a cloud diary?

How can you add challenge?

Children can be encouraged to:

> be more systematic and precise in how they collect data

> distinguish between opinion and evidence

> recognise that data sets can be connected without it being a causal relationship

> recognise anomalies in their data and begin to explain them.

RESEARCH | Introduction

What is Research?

Scientists do research to investigate hypotheses and answer scientific questions. However, in this book we use the term as it is usually used in primary science, that is to describe enquires where the answer is found using secondary sources.

There are lots of questions that are impossible or unsafe for children to answer using first hand experience, such as what lives in Antarctica, or how glass is made. When researching using secondary sources they can learn:

> to compare and evaluate information from different sources

> to distinguish fact from opinion and recognise conflicting evidence and bias

> to recognise questions that don't have definite answers.

Researching something that interests them enables children to answer their own questions and stimulates them to ask and answer more questions. This type of enquiry provides good opportunities to practice and develop aspects of mathematics, English and ICT.

The table on the next page shows examples of starting points for research.

Getting started

Opportunities for research-based enquiries arise where children wonder about the world beyond their classroom or speculate about things they have observed. Their questions can range from the simple factual (e.g. How cold is it on Neptune?) to how and why questions that require complex explanations. Children will ask many of these questions spontaneously, provoked by their own curiosity and exploration of the world around them. Hands-on experiences often lead to research.

However not all research will be initiated by children. You can also plan opportunities for children to extend their enquiries beyond first hand investigations and to link their experiences to bigger scientific questions. Research can complement children's practical investigating, enabling them to make broader generalisations and providing a stimulus for collecting first hand data (e.g. children who find out that the male and female human pelvis are different shapes may then measure classmates to look for other gender differences, such as foot size or arm length). Visits and visitors are a good source of both answers and questions.

Research is a good way to answer children's why questions – but it may not be the only way. Before turning to secondary sources to find the answer, encourage them to think about whether there are other ways that they could find out. Could they propose an idea to test instead? For example, they may be wondering why we usually find woodlice under stones and logs, and they could find out using reference books or the internet. Alternatively they could carry out an investigation into what conditions woodlice prefer, and then use their observations to suggest possible explanations for why woodlice are found in certain places. Research using secondary sources could then be a follow up to their investigation.

Starting points for Research using Secondary Sources

LIVING THINGS

Animals

Why do birds migrate? Which birds migrate the furthest?

What is the difference between a cold and warm-blooded animal?

What attracts bees to our flowers?

Why do different animals live in different places?

Why do snails and other animals living around the school behave in the way that they do?

What is the impact of climate change on plants and animals?

Are zoos a good thing?

Plants

How do we measure the height of this tree? How can we work out how old our hedge is?

Do any plants grow without soil? How do plants survive in very wet or dry places?

How do our plants get their food? Why did our flowers wilt?

Where does our food come from? How do we get chocolate? How much bread does a field of wheat make?

How are different types of flour made?

Ourselves

What happens when we go to the dentist / opticians / baby clinic?

What difference would it make if I eat a vegetarian diet?

How much sleep do we need?

What are the healthiest ways of cooking our food?

What happens if we go without some foods? What happens if we eat too much of some foods?

How are medicines invented? What diseases can we be vaccinated against?

Why are some people better athletes than others? How do athletes train?

Why do we sweat?

What do different kinds of teeth do? How does tooth decay happen?

How tall is the tallest person? How do airlines decide how much legroom passengers need?

How are fingerprints used to identify people? What other features can be used?

Microorganisms

Are all microbes harmful to us? What do germs do? How do they spread?

How can we make compost and how is it useful?

Why do we use yeast in bread? How can we make our own yoghurt?

What did Louis Pasteur and Alexander Fleming discover? What difference have their discoveries made to our lives?

MATERIALS AND THEIR USES

Change of state

What's the purpose of insulation in the school?

How are candles made? Some things change when they are heated. How do we make use of this?

How does a thermometer work?

How does a barometer work?

How can seawater be made drinkable?

Use of materials

Why do tea bags come in different shapes and sizes?

How are furnishing fabrics made flame retardant / water proof and why?

Can any natural materials be used raw or do they all need processing in some way?

When was glass / plastic first used? What was the impact on us of its invention?

FORCES, ENERGY AND MOVEMENT

Buildings

What are different types of bridge called? Which are the strongest?

Why don't cranes fall over?

How did the Egyptians move the heavy rocks to build the pyramids?

Transport

How do submarines work? How does a hot air balloon fly?

When is a helicopter more useful than an aeroplane? Why?

Energy

What's the difference between renewable and non-renewable energy?

How can we use water to generate energy?

Electricity and magnetism

What did Michael Faraday and Humphrey Davy invent?

How much energy do low energy light bulbs save us?

EARTH AND BEYOND

Moon and stars

Why does the Moon's appearance change? What is a lunar eclipse?

What is a star? How does a telescope work? What do astronomers do?

What do astrologers do? Do their predictions work?

Time

How can we tell the time without clocks?

What do we think would happen if the Earth started to rotate more slowly?

How does a sundial work?

Rocks and soils

Where does salt come from? Which rocks are the oldest? Which rocks are formed by volcanic action? How are caves formed? How are fossils formed? Where are most fossils found? What was important about Mary Anning's discoveries and research?

What do archaeologists and diamond hunters need to know about rocks?

How are bricks made? Are all bricks the same? Why do we use bricks to build houses?

Why is an oil spill such bad news for wild life and so difficult to clear up?

SOUND

How do wind chimes work?

How is sound measured? What is the loudest noise ever recorded? What can a dog hear that we can't?

LIGHT

What are optical illusions? How can we produce them? How far does the brightest light shine?

What can children do when they research?

Ideas for activities

There are many different contexts in which children can carry out research enquiries. Suggestions for these are given in the Starting Points table on the previous two pages, and in each of the four activities described in detail later.

Developing scientific skills and understanding

Research enquiries give children opportunities to practice some of the skills that are often less well developed in practical investigations. As the need to plan and collect data first hand is removed, the focus shifts to analysis and communication. Research enquiries provide good contexts for children to use and develop the skills of interpreting and looking critically at evidence, drawing conclusions and explaining, and presenting information in different ways. They will also need to develop the skills of note-taking from written materials, the spoken word and visual media such as video clips. These skills provide a distinctive way for children to develop their understanding of scientific ideas. As children develop their skills, the depth and range of their understanding should also increase.

Children will become more independent as they move from single, simple information sources to choosing from a range of sources and the use of multiple information sources to answer a question. They will progress from using simple secondary data presented in familiar ways, to data from less familiar settings presented in unfamiliar formats. They will move from accepting information from any source as correct, to thinking about how data was obtained in order to decide how trustworthy it is.

The questions children investigate in research enquiries often lead them into an important but sometimes neglected part of science enquiry, namely finding out about how people use science in their jobs, and forming opinions about scientific developments and the moral or ethical issues that arise.

Children working with secondary data may re-present it (e.g. by drawing a graph from a table of data) in order to interpret it. Research provides opportunities to take notes, make mind maps, summarise information, model ideas using diagrams or physical models, and present information for different audiences and in different ways. These enquiries may lead to posters, songs, extended writing, spoken or ICT presentations, as well as simple answers and conclusions. Through research using secondary sources children will develop and practice many of the literacy, numeracy and ICT skills needed in science.

The grid on page 112 shows the progression of skills that children use when engaging in research. You can use the grid to ensure that there is sufficient challenge in the research enquiries that you plan.

Encouraging talk and questioning

Children can be very good at asking questions that can't be answered though first hand experience.

Daisy wants to know where all the stars go in the daytime.

Sunita asked how long crocodiles live.

They may suggest ways to find out, but will need some help to identify possible sources of information. You can help children to focus their questions. Get them to talk about how to find answers using secondary sources.

Shall we ask Jaspar's Aunt Soraya? She knows about stars.

Let's see if there is a book about crocodiles in the library.

Where could we look on the computer? What will we do if different websites say different things?

The amount of information available can be overwhelming. Encourage children to discuss what they want to find out and refine their questions. Encourage them to talk to each other about what they have discovered and how to present it, rather than simply copying chunks of text. Encourage children to be on the lookout for vested interests and bias.

Where has the information come from? Is it up to date?

Where did they find their evidence? Do you agree with their interpretation?

Might the author be biased?

By giving children opportunities to talk with you and each other, they can be encouraged to think about how they will raise more focused questions and find answers to these questions. They can share the information that they find and, with your support, learn to make decisions about its value and reliability and how to record and communicate their findings.

What are the possible outcomes?

Research enquiries will lead to different kinds of outcomes that will provide rich assessment evidence:

> extended writing, notes or videos about some aspect of science

> representations and comparisons of information and ideas (e.g. models, concept maps)

> tables, graphs and other visual means of presenting data

> presentations to others that are spoken or involve the use of posters, songs, poems, drama, role play, news reports, powerpoint, videos or podcasts.

Research: Skills Progression Grid

	Plan	Do	Review
Foundation	• I am curious about things in my surroundings • With help, I ask questions that I can answer using secondary sources	• I listen carefully • I know that information in books and electronic media can be used to answer questions • I find pictures of things • I talk to people about what they do and how things work	• I talk about things I found out
Early primary	• I ask questions about how things are and the way they work • With help, I make suggestions about how to find things out	• I use simple books and electronic media to find things out • I ask questions to find out what people do and how things work • I record in words and pictures what I found out	• I begin to use scientific language to talk about what I found out • I talk about whether the information source was useful • I give an opinion about some things I found out
Middle primary	• I talk about how things are and the way they work and decide when questions can be answered by research using secondary sources	• I use information sources to find the information I need • I use someone else's data • I record what I found out in my own words • I present information in different ways	• I draw conclusions from what I found out from different sources • I talk about what the information and data means using some scientific language • I suggest ways to improve how I find out and use information
Late primary	• I recognise when research using secondary sources will help to answer my questions • I decide which sources of information might answer my questions	• I use relevant information and data from a range of secondary sources • I recognise how data has been obtained • I start to notice when information and data is biased or based on opinions rather than facts • I present my findings in suitable formats	• I draw valid conclusions from my research • I talk about and explain my research using scientific knowledge and understanding • I evaluate how well my research has answered my questions • I recognise that some scientific questions may not have been answered definitively

SCIENTISTS IN THE COMMUNITY

Many people in the community use science in what that they do (e.g. optician, nurse, hairdresser, chef in a pizzeria, gardener or farmer). Contact with these people is a great way for children to begin to develop their research skills. We focus on just one of these, the gardener, which you can use as a template for other people in the community.

It would be ideal if the children could visit a local garden or garden centre. You may be able to organise for another member of staff to take children in small groups for a short visit, if you prefer, rather than arrange a whole class trip. This may be easier for the gardener too! Alternatively you could invite a local gardener or garden centre worker into school. If children work in small groups, each group could be challenged to find out certain things that they report back to their classmates. By focusing on one or two things to find out at a time, the children can steadily build up a secure understanding about the role of science in the person's job.

Health and Safety Notes

- *Follow your school's guidelines for working out of doors. Children must wash their hands after handling plants or planting medium and after visiting a garden or garden centre. Ensure that all plants and seeds are safe to use and are not poisonous or treated with fungicide. Warn children about the dangers of eating seeds and plant material.*

Getting started

You can build on children's spontaneous observations and questions

Lots of children will have contact with adults who grow things.

> *My dad's growing some flowers. I like the yellow ones.*
>
> *We went to the garden centre on Sunday and bought some seeds to grow.*
>
> *My aunty has got lots of vegetables in her garden. I'm going with my big sister to pick some after school.*

You can ask questions to focus their observations

You may need to go outside or provide resources to help children think about these questions.

> *We've got some flowers in the school garden. Shall we go and look at them? Where do you think they came from?*
>
> *I wonder what we do with the seeds? How could we find out?*
>
> *Where do you think the vegetables came from?*
>
> *Do you think your aunty will come in to show us what she grows and tell us more about them?*

You can provide your own starting points

Your role will be to pose a problem that raises possibilities for research.

> *There was a free packet of seeds on the magazine I bought yesterday, but I don't know what to do with them? How can we find out?*
>
> *We are having a summer fair and I think we could grow some plants to sell. We've never grown plants in this class before. I wonder who could help us to grow some really good plants?*

WHAT CAN CHILDREN DO?

IDEAS FOR ACTIVITIES

Children can:

> think of things they want to find out when they visit the garden or garden centre, or a gardener comes to school
> talk to a gardener and find out what they do
> collect seeds, plant pots, etc.
> observe plants growing, talk about what they notice and take photographs to help them tell others what they saw
> collect leaflets about growing plants and, with help, get information from seed packets
> 'help you' to create a garden centre in the role play area and, with help, make notices for the garden centre
> pretend to be a gardener and role play the things that they found out about what a gardener does

> grow plants from seeds or cuttings
> work in the garden centre to look after their plants
> invite a gardener to their classroom to share what they have done in their class garden centre.

DEVELOPING SKILLS AND UNDERSTANDING

Give children lots of opportunities to:

> look carefully during their research visit and, with supervision, talk to the people who work there
> make a record of what they see and share with others what they found out
> talk with each other about their experiences when they visited the garden centre or talked to a gardener
> talk about being a gardener and how they might start their own mini gardens, either at school or home
> look at books and other sources of information about growing things
> develop and use key vocabulary (e.g. find out, ask, question, job, tools, equipment, growing, seeds, plants, soil, water).

Encouraging talk and questioning

Try to help children to raise their own questions by giving them time to talk together and share what they already know about growing things. You can help them to turn the ideas that they share into questions to explore.

Megan and Peri said that they thought you had to put sticks in for the beans to grow up, but they didn't know if they needed sticks for other plants.

Carly and Sam said that when they planted seeds, some of them didn't grow but they didn't know why.

Children may be able to suggest ways of finding out but may need help deciding what to use to do their research.

What else do you think we can do to find out as well as growing things for ourselves? Perhaps we can ask the gardener what she thinks.

Talk to your partner about the most exciting thing you found out.

What did you find out that will help us to grow some plants?

You can help them to raise more questions to investigate in different ways by being puzzled by something that they found out.

I've got another question. The gardener said that she puts fertiliser on the plants to help them grow. I want to ask her if we put lots of fertiliser on a plant will it grow really big?

What do you want to find out?

What are the possible outcomes?

Researching growing things leads to different kinds of outcomes

These can provide rich assessment evidence of their developing skills and understanding.

For example:

> what they say to each other, and you, about what they want to find out about what a gardener does and what they have learned

> what they say to the people they visit or who visit them

> what they say about what they have seen the gardener do

> what they say about what the gardener has said

> their drawings or photographs of the gardener, how to grow plants and the plants growing

> the ideas that they share after their visits

> how they arrange and use the role play area as a garden centre

> how they grow and care for their plants

> how they compare their own experience with what they hear about from others or see in books.

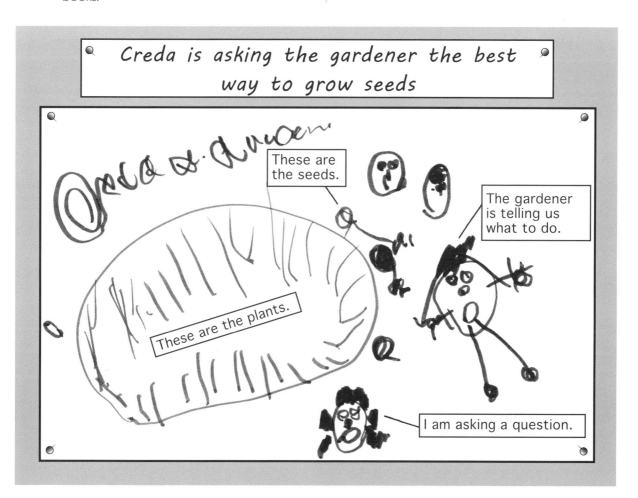

Creda is asking the gardener the best way to grow seeds

These are the seeds.

The gardener is telling us what to do.

These are the plants.

I am asking a question.

Questions that can lead to other types of enquiry

Questions that children may ask (or you could ask them)

Do little seeds grow into little plants? Do big seeds grow into big plants?

Where's the best place for growing plants?

Can we go outside to find out?

Will all the plants grow under the tree?

Can we go outside to find out?

Will all the plants be ready to sell at the summer fayre?

What will our plants look like when they grow? Will they all look the same?

How can you add challenge?

Children can be encouraged to:

> think about what science the gardener is using

> talk about why they think some plants didn't grow and share their ideas with the gardener

> with help, create a picture guide to growing plants

> look at photographs of plants growing, in books or that other children have taken, and describe what they see and what they think is happening

> suggest other people who use science in the community that they can find out about.

MAKING A CHOCOLATE BAR

Chocolate is generally a popular topic with children and an easy way to explore melting and solidifying. It can be a rich starting point for all types of scientific enquiry, including research. Chocolate comes in many different types: dark chocolate, milk chocolate, white chocolate, drinking chocolate, bars, sweets, cakes and Easter eggs. Exploring a selection of different types of chocolate is a good way of generating questions as a lead in to this activity.

Some of these questions (e.g. which is your favourite, which melts fastest, or how can you sort all these chocolate bars into groups?) can be answered by practical activity. Other questions, (e.g. how chocolate is made, where it comes from and what goes into chocolate bars) require research using secondary sources. The end point can be creating an interesting chocolate bar and gives a good sense of purpose to this activity.

> ### *Health and Safety Notes*
> - *If any of the chocolate is to be eaten, follow the school's food preparation and hygiene guidelines, including keeping surfaces clean and washing hands. Chocolate should be melted over a suitable container of warm water and the process supervised closely. Check for any nut allergies and plan the activity accordingly.*

Getting started

You can build on children's spontaneous observations and questions

You could let the children know they will be exploring chocolate and make a note of any questions that they can think of ready for when you start.

> I went to a shop that makes chocolates at the weekend. I've brought you one to try. Do you like it?
>
> I've got a new chocolate bar that was advertised on the television. It tastes lovely.
>
> Why is it called milk chocolate? You can't drink it.

You can ask questions to focus their observations

Try to use questions that focus children on researching chocolate.

> Did you see the chocolates being made? What did they use to make the chocolates? What kinds of chocolate did you see?
>
> What's in the chocolate bar? I wonder how they decide what to use?
>
> Who has tasted different kinds of chocolate? What were they like?

You can provide your own starting points

Your role will be to pose a problem that raises possibilities for research.

> Look at all these different chocolate bars. I wonder how new chocolate bars are invented? I wonder who first invented chocolate?
>
> I bought my gran a box of chocolates for her birthday. She loves them. She says that when she was little she hardly ever had chocolate. I wonder why?
>
> I'm not sure where chocolate comes from. Does anyone know? I wonder how we could find out?

> Last weekend I went to a big greenhouse in a botanic garden. A part of one of the trees is used for making chocolate! Can you find out what it is and how it is used?
>
> My sister has stopped eating chocolate because she says it's not healthy. Do you think she's right?

WHAT CAN CHILDREN DO?

IDEAS FOR ACTIVITIES

Children can:

> talk about what they know about chocolate and decide what to do to find out and how to find out

> visit a shop, or collect chocolate bars, to look at the different kinds there are and the different ingredients used

> ask a shopkeeper which is the most popular type of chocolate bar and talk about what they find out. Do girls, boys, men and women like different types?

> invite into school someone from a chocolate shop, or someone who makes chocolate cakes

> work together to design a chocolate bar and its ingredients and then make it

> evaluate the chocolate bars by sharing them with others and getting feedback

> research and design packaging for the chocolate bar and produce an advert for the chocolate bar

> use a book, video or website to find out how chocolate is made

> use pictures to make a flow chart of the process

> talk about the sort of places where cocoa trees grow and plot them on a map

> talk to a dentist or nurse about eating chocolate and, with help, make an 'Eating chocolate and staying healthy' poster.

DEVELOPING SKILLS AND UNDERSTANDING

Give children lots of opportunities to:

> talk to each other about what they want to find out and how they might do this

> use a variety of information sources

> share with each other the things they've discovered

> present their findings in different ways (e.g. pictures, reports, graphs)

> develop and use key vocabulary (e.g. grow, plant, cocoa, milk, beans, mix, melt, roast, powder, diet).

Encouraging talk and questioning

Encourage the children to share what they already know about chocolate.

With your talk partner, can you think of two things that you know about chocolate and two more things that you would like to know?

Does anyone know the answer to someone else's question?

Encourage the children to think about the best way to answer their questions.

How can you find out more about chocolate? Talk together about what you think.

Do we need to ask someone? Who shall we invite into our class?

We can go to the chocolate shop. Can you think of the most important questions to ask when we are there?

Can anyone find a book that we could look in?

Plan with your partner how to make your chocolate bar. How will you decide what to use and how to make it?

When they have finished their research, encourage them to talk about what they have found out.

Now you have got your information, share what you have found with another pair. Is there anything that you don't agree about?

How will we decide what makes a good chocolate bar? Talk together about your ideas.

Encourage them to raise more questions.

Look at all the things we have already found out about chocolate. Are there any other things you would still like to know?

I'll gather your ideas on the whiteboard.

What are the possible outcomes?

Researching chocolate leads to different kinds of outcomes

These can provide rich assessment evidence of their developing skills and understanding.

For example:

> what they say to each other, and you, about how they found answers to their questions about chocolate

> notes and other records made after investigating chocolate bars and carrying out other research

> graphs or other records of people's preferences

> descriptions of what they find out about how and where cocoa is grown and how chocolate is made, and how they present the information they find

> the chocolate bar that they make, and how they describe and evaluate it

> a demonstration video of how to make a chocolate bar

> the content of their advertising or healthy eating poster

> the recommendations they make about eating chocolate as part of a balanced diet.

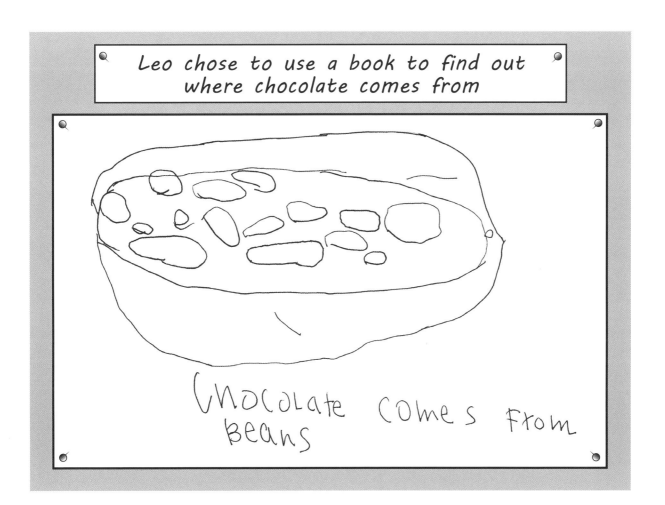

Leo chose to use a book to find out where chocolate comes from

Chocolate comes from beans

Questions that can lead to other types of enquiry

Questions that children may ask (or you could ask them)

I left my chocolate in the fridge and now it smells of onions! What happened? How can we stop it happening again?

Does all chocolate take the same time to melt? Does chocolate taste the same after it has been melted?

I wonder which is the most popular chocolate bar in our class?

How can we sort different types of chocolate into groups?

Will my friends be able to recognise the different types of chocolate in a taste test?

How can you add challenge?

Children can be encouraged to:

> select information from a wide range of sources, including suitable internet sites

> use a graphic organiser to show the different ingredients of chocolate and the effect if one ingredient is missing

> think about the environmental impact of cocoa beans being flown across the world so that we can eat chocolate.

RESEARCHING EARTH IN SPACE

Astronomy is a fascinating subject but not an easy one to investigate at first hand in primary schools. However the internet and downloaded TV programmes can bring the night sky vividly into classrooms; observatories offer a warm welcome to visiting groups; the experiences of astronauts are well documented in film and books; children can experience the beauty of the constellations in a mobile planetarium in their school hall; there are plenty of excellent books about space; and there are some brilliant museums and space centres to visit.

With a little advance planning, you can provide an enquiry-based approach with a balance between first hand practical experience and finding out using secondary sources, to learn about the Earth, Sun and Moon, planets, galaxies, time and space.

Health and Safety Notes

- *Make sure that children do not look directly at the Sun and do not look at the Sun through an optical instrument.*

Getting started

You can build on children's spontaneous observations and questions

Children are surround by sources of ideas related to the Earth and beyond. You could let them know that you are going to do a project on this and start collecting their observations and questions.

> I'd like to be an astronaut.
>
> When we went camping we saw millions of stars.
>
> I saw Venus last night. Our neighbour has a telescope in the garden and I had a look.

You can ask questions to focus their observations

Use questions that focus on research-based enquiry.

> What does an astronaut do? What do you know about them?
>
> Do you recognise any of the stars? Do you know any of their names?
>
> What did Venus look like? How did you know where to look? Does anyone know anything about Venus?

You can provide your own starting points

Your role will be to pose a problem that raises possibilities for research.

> Let's go on a night-time walk on our school trip. If we take some mats we can lie on our backs and look at the sky. What do you think we'll see?
>
> We can visit an observatory to look through the telescopes and talk to the astronomers. What questions would you like to ask?
>
> Why do you think the stars come out at night? Where do they go to during the day?

> When I was your age my grandad told me that when I was grown up, everyone would be going to the Moon for their holidays. It hasn't happened yet! I wonder why?
>
> A friend of mine has lent me her telescope. Can you find out how it works? I wonder who invented telescopes?

WHAT CAN CHILDREN DO?

IDEAS FOR ACTIVITIES

Children can:

> complete a KWHL grid (things I Know, things I Want to know, How I will find out, things I have Learnt)

> create a question board, and add answers to it as they find out more information

> talk about which questions they think will have definite answers and which are more uncertain

> visit an observatory to look through a telescope, or look at images from online telescopes

> explore the night sky in a planetarium, using a star map to identify the constellations

> talk to an astronomer

> create a tourist guide to the planets or make a holiday brochure for the Moon

> read about the Apollo Moon landings and the Apollo 13 problems, and act out scenes from inside the space rocket or on the Moon

> compile a list of top tips for astronauts (e.g. what to eat, how to cope with weightlessness) or write entries for an astronaut's diary

> hot seat as an astronomer or astronaut, and answer questions about what they do and why

DEVELOPING SKILLS AND UNDERSTANDING

Give children lots of opportunities to:

> talk with each other about what they want to find out and use a variety of secondary sources to answer their questions

> raise more questions based on what they've observed or found out

> talk with each other about what they've done and compare their findings

> present their findings in a variety of ways, such as written reports, posters, diagrams, annotated drawings, graphic organisers, powerpoint, video clips or podcasts

> develop and use key vocabulary (e.g space, atmosphere, temperature, orbit, day, year, planet, galaxy, star, constellation).

Encouraging talk and questioning

Encourage children to talk together to explore their ideas and think about their previous experience of the Moon, the planets, stars or astronomical events.

Talk to your partner about where you might see the North Star. How could we check?

You have all seen the Moon. Talk about what you think it looks like. How could you check your ideas?

In your group can you work out which planets are close to us? What are they like?

Talk about what you think the stars are made of. Does anyone know? Where can we get some information?

Help them to think about the questions they would like to research further and to think about the best place to find answers.

You've created a great set of questions here about the planets. How can we find out the answers? We can check with the astronomer when we visit the observatory. What else can we do?

Lots of children want to know the names of stars. I wonder if we could find a star map?

Lots of you have written questions about what it's like being an astronaut. I wonder if we can find a website that will answer them? Maybe we can find an astronaut's diary or biography somewhere? What else can we do?

Encourage them to talk about what they have found out and think of new questions to research.

I'd like you to share what you have found with another group and ask each other questions about it. Are there questions that you can't answer? Write them in your notebook so we can think about them later.

Are there other things you would still like to know?

What are the possible outcomes?

Researching the Earth in space leads to different kinds of outcomes

These can provide rich assessment evidence of their developing skills and understanding.

For example:

> what they say to each other, and you, about how they decided on their questions about the Earth in space and found the answers

> how they use a variety of information sources to answer their questions

> their interpretation and presentation of the data they have found

> their tourist or holiday guides to the planets or the Moon

> the way they act out things that they have found out (e.g. Apollo 13)

> their top tips for astronauts

> the content of their guides to the planets or night sky

> what they say when they hot seat as an astronomer

> their evaluation of how they have answered their questions.

Isobel and Ed chose a graphic organiser to present their research about planets

Rocky Planets	Compare and Contrast	Gas Planets
All Small	Size	All bigger than rocky ones
Closer	Distance from Sun	Further away
Mainly nitrigen + Oxygen	Atmosphere	Mainly hydrogen and helium
Some you can Some are too hot.	Possible to visit from Earth	Can't land, Will go right through
The two closer planets are very hot.	Temperature	Bellow zero
brown, red, blue.	How they look	Rings around them

How did you find out?

Space books, Internet and Astronomy club at School

Questions that can lead to other types of enquiry

The Moon is a different shape today compared to last week. I wonder if it always changes in the same way?

Does the Sun always come up at the same time of day? Does it always come up in the same place?

I found the Big Dipper in the sky last night. Is it always in the same place?

How can we make a sundial?

How can you add challenge?

Children can be encouraged to:

> ask questions about how the data they are using was collected

> compare what people knew about the night sky 500 years ago with now

> find more creative ways to share their findings (e.g. write or contribute to blog)

> find out about stone circles and how these link with astronomy

> think about and discuss how scientific and technological developments help us to learn more about space.

RESEARCHING SPORT

All children should be encouraged to participate in and enjoy sport. Investigating how our bodies move and grow offers opportunities for enquiries that involve children in first hand collection and analysis of data. Sport has an extensive and accessible database of information about athletes, world records, fitness, training and diets that children can interrogate. They can also look at local and school-based data, such as how many people use the local swimming pool, how many children play in teams, what children do at playtime, and so on.

A major sporting event or a local event that is in the news can provide an obvious context for children to find out about athletes and what their bodies do. Research and practical activity can easily be linked. For example, children might compare their performance with that of the athletes, look at how age and performance are related, or try to find out if performance in one sport is linked with performance in another.

Health and Safety Notes

- *Check whether there are any individual health issues (such as asthma) before getting the children to engage in any sporting activity.*

Getting started

You can build on children's spontaneous observations and questions

Children engage in a wide range of sports. Any of these could provide good starting points.

We went to watch my aunty run in the London Marathon.

On the netball team the goal attack scores so many goals because she's so tall and can throw the ball well.

I go swimming twice a week. My mum reckons it's good for me.

You can ask questions to focus their observations

Use questions that focus on research-based enquiry.

Do you have to train much to run a marathon? Could anybody run a marathon? Does everyone take the same amount of time to run the marathon? What happens at the end of the marathon if people are really tired? Do you have to eat extra food so that you can run that far?

Are goal attacks always tall? Is there anything else that makes a good goal attack? Do they run fast?

Is swimming good exercise for our bodies? What's especially good about it?

You can provide your own starting points

Your role will be to pose a problem that raises possibilities for research.

Look at this picture of how much an Olympic rower eats every day! Why do you think they eat so much?

We found out that the tallest people in our class could jump the furthest. Do you think it's the same for the other classes? Shall we ask them to find out and give us their data? Do you think all good jumpers are tall?

Look at this newspaper headline: 'Council plans free swimming for old people'. Do you think this is a good idea?

My Dad was telling me about the first time someone ran a mile in less than four minutes. What's the world record now? Why has it changed?

WHAT CAN CHILDREN DO?

IDEAS FOR ACTIVITIES

Children can:

> identify key questions that they want to answer
> attend a local sporting event and interview participants, then write a report of the event with photographs
> hot seat as a professional athlete and answer questions about their training
> design fitness regimes for people of different ages
> find out how technology helps athletes (e.g. a sprinter who runs on prosthetic limbs, treadmills that simulate uphill running, new fabrics for swimming costumes, new designs for running shoes)
> plan a diet for a marathon runner, cyclist or swimmer
> write a poem about running in a marathon, or complete a marathon runner's diary
> compare sprint and long distance records from now, 10, and 50 years ago, and explain why they think runners are getting faster
> compare humans with other animals (e.g. in sprinting, swimming or jumping)
> produce a concept map about sports and fitness.

DEVELOPING SKILLS AND UNDERSTANDING

Give children lots of opportunities to:

> talk to each other, and you, about the things they want to find out
> identify which questions can't be answered by investigation, and decide where and how they will find the information they need
> check their findings with another source and decide whether the data are valid
> decide how to present data in new ways, such as tables, bar graphs, pie charts
> talk with each other about what they've done and compare their fact sheets with others
> develop and use key vocabulary (e.g. fitness, diet, training, muscles, pulse rate, heart rate, breathing, sweating).

Encouraging talk and questioning

Children enjoy talking about sporting events, from school sports to the Olympics. Encourage them to do their own research, by talking to participants in sporting events or collecting data from newspapers and websites. Help them to work together to focus on what they want to find out.

Work with your partner to decide which sport you are going to research. What exactly do you want to know? Which are your key questions? Where do you think you will find the information?

Here's a KWHL grid (things I think I Know, things I Want to know, How I will find out, things I have Learnt). Work on it with a partner. How will you find out the answers to your questions? Which questions do you think you should answer first?

There are some special things inside this bag. Take it to your table and have a peep inside. What can you find out about what's in there?

Give them time to talk together to plan how they will find out the answers. You may need to give them some guidance about how to carry out the research to help them learn new ways of finding out.

I've found some interesting tables of information on the internet. Look at them together. How will they help to answer your questions? What else can you do to find out?

There are lots of different information sources that you can use. It isn't possible for everybody to find out everything, so your team will have to think about who does what.

How will you organise the information that you collect? What are the different possibilities? Talk together to decide.

After the children have finished their research, encourage them to talk about what they have found out.

You have all found out different information. I want you to split up and pair with a person you haven't worked with yet to find out something new.

What can we do with what we have found out about these different sports? Could we produce a guide to help people decide which sport would be a good one for them? Have you got other ideas?

What are the possible outcomes?

Researching sport leads to different kinds of outcomes

These can provide rich assessment evidence of their developing skills and understanding.

For example:

> what they say to each other, and you, about what they want to find out and where they look for the information about science and sport

> how they presented data in their own words and in different formats

> what they say when they hot seat as an athlete

> their written and oral descriptions of how different athletes train and prepare, the skills and talents they need, and the emotions they may experience

> their fact sheets about how science helps athletes

> their diet plan for a sports person

> the content of a marathon runner's diary or poem

> the conclusions that they draw about changes in sporting achievement and how science and other factors might have helped

> their evaluation of what they have produced.

Paulo decided to use the Internet to carry out his research into running shoes

Part 2 Changes in running shoes

In 1900 a new process called vulcanisation produced the first proper running shoes. The process helped rubber and cloth to stick together to make the shoes strong, comfortable, light and reduced the impact on runners' heels. Unfortunately the shoes were not very durable so wore out too quickly.

Durability as well as density, strength, elasticity and stability are important properties for running shoes. Research into new materials looks for good combinations of each of these. It also has to take into account the ways people run (see Part 3 research into the way runners run) and the best ways to support feet and cushion runners' heels.

INSOLE
(ethylene vinyl acetate (EVA)) padding

OUTSOLE
(carbon rubber or blown rubber) extra absorption

UPPERS
(artificial suede, nylon, leather) tough and flexible

MIDSOLE
(polyurethane with gel or liquid silicone, or polyurethane foam) shock absorber

More information at: www.madehow.com/Volume-1/Running-Shoe.html

Questions that can lead to other types of enquiry

Questions that children may ask (or you could ask them)

Can anyone be an Olympic athlete?

I wonder if more young people or old people use our local pool?

Do the fastest runners in the class have the fastest pulse rate, before and after exercise?

Which type of exercise will make my heart beat fastest?

We didn't see much of a pattern between height and jumping distance. Will it be the same in another class?

Is it true that people with the longest legs run the quickest? What about other things, like whether you can throw better if you are older?

How can you add challenge?

Children can be encouraged to:

> ask questions that require more detailed information

> explain why some questions don't have definitive answers

> think about how the data they are using were collected and how valid they are

> describe some technological and scientific developments in sport

> think about some ethical and moral issues in sport

> identify reasons why different sources may provide conflicting data.

FAIR TESTING I Introduction

What is Fair Testing?

Fair test enquiries enable children to explore causal relationships between variables that they can change. Fair tests involve changing one variable and observing the effect this has on another variable, whilst keeping everything else the same. For example, how does changing the height of a ramp affect how quickly a toy car rolls down it. Children can answer questions by collecting data to identify, and then explain, the relationship between the variables. Fair tests are suitable when variables can be changed, so they are very useful for finding out about materials and physical phenomena. They are not suitable when we can't change something in a systematic way (e.g. experiments on humans or the weather). In these situations other types of enquiries need to be used.

Sometimes children misunderstand the word 'fair' to mean equitable, such as whether their group behaved in a fair manner to each other, rather than whether they kept all the important variables the same. They might also talk about making investigations fair when what they mean is choosing a way to collect data that will give valid results.

The table on the next page shows examples of starting points for fair testing.

Getting started

Opportunities for fair tests arise where children notice that one thing has an effect on another, (e.g. children slide more on a slippery floor in socks than in trainers, or one type of kitchen towel is advertised as soaking up more liquid than another). Often it is the observation that one thing is 'better' than another that leads to a fair test. This may happen spontaneously, or you can provide a stimulus to provoke children's observations and questions.

Your task is to help children identify what is the difference that they have noticed (e.g. faster melting chocolate) and to explore all the variables that might affect it (amount of chocolate, stirring, temperature, container, percentage of cocoa solids, etc). When they have decided which variable to investigate, children need to decide how they will measure or observe the effects (e.g. how does the percentage of cocoa solids affect how quickly the chocolate melts?). Then they need to control all the other important variables to ensure that the test is fair. Children will need lots of support to learn this process of generating a fair test question, identifying variables, planning how to carry out a fair test and collecting and analysing evidence. They will need to be able to recognise when tests are fair before they can set up fair tests on their own.

A fair test may lead to more fair tests with different variables. Fair testing may lead children to ask questions that can't be answered by fair tests, and go on to other types of enquiries such as **pattern seeking** or **observing over time**. Sometimes they may go on to carry out **research** using secondary sources to seek explanations for the relationships they observed.

Starting points for Fair Tests

LIVING THINGS

Animals

I think different animals behave in different ways. How does changing the colour of a food affect the number of birds visiting our bird table?

Do bees prefer red or yellow flowers?

Do woodlice move more in dark or light conditions?

Plants

Do we need to make sure that we plant the seeds the right way up? How does changing the way we plant them make a difference to how they germinate? What else can we change?

Will seeds germinate in salty or oily water?

If we don't look after our plants properly we think they will die. How does changing the amount of water make a difference to how well they grow? What else can we change?

Ourselves

The dentist said some drinks harm your teeth. Which drinks are the most harmful to us?

When I go to gymnastics the trainer says that what you do to your body makes a difference. How does changing duration and intensity of exercise affect our pulse rates and recovery time?

Microorganisms

The paper changed really quickly when we left a piece on the soil. What makes a difference to how quickly things rot when we leave them outside?

Nana says wrapping things in cling film stops them going mouldy. What stops things going mouldy? (**Safety:** Do not use meat or fish)

Some bread is flat and some is big and fluffy. How does changing the amount of water, sugar or the temperature affect the amount our bread rises?

MATERIALS AND THEIR USES

Washing

The school's sports kits are very dirty. What is the best way to get them clean?

What difference does the type of soap make?

What about the temperature of the water?

Does our washing dry faster on a sunny or windy day?

Bubbles

We're making some bubble mixture. What happens if we change any of the ingredients in the recipe? How does changing the mixture affect how long our bubbles last?

Do bigger bubbles float higher?

Do small bubbles travel faster?

Food

We're making cup cakes for the school fair. Will people think they taste different if we make the cakes different colours?

Fitness for purpose

Which are the best:

- ways to pack eggs, containers for hot drinks, materials for a carrier bag, toothpastes
- coats for keeping us warm, glues to hold things together, soaps for removing stains
- materials for curtains / bedspread / chair cover / table cloth, tissues for a runny nose
- kitchen towels for mopping up spills, tea bags, umbrellas, washing powders
- ways to build a wall with bricks, ways to make tea, wrappers for chocolate
- rocks for a statue for our garden, pens for writing on the notice board by the school gate
- ways to stop food drying out, ways to stop our snowman melting, ways to make the ice melt faster, ways to make washing dry faster?

FORCES, ENERGY AND MOVEMENT

Friction

It's icy outside. Which of our shoes have the most grip?

Falling

Do heavier people fall further when they bungee jump?

How does the shape of the leaves affect the way they fall?

What will affect how well our paper spinners fall?

Movement

What affects how far our toy car travels when it rolls down a ramp?

How does changing our parachutes affect how our toy figures fall?

What makes a difference to how far our balloon rocket can go?

Electricity and magnetism

How does changing parts of our circuit affect the brightness of the bulb?

Which is the best magnet for our fridge?

SOUND

Instruments

How does the sound change if we put more water in the bottle? I think the sound gets deeper.

How does changing the amount of water change the pitch? Does it matter if I blow or strike the bottle?

How does changing the size of a musical instrument affect the pitch or loudness of the sound?

What shape or material makes the best ear trumpet?

Sound insulation

Which is the best material for muffling sound?

What's the best way to protect our ears from loud sounds?

LIGHT

Reflecting and blocking light

We want to put a star on the magician's wand for the pantomime. Which material makes the best reflector?

Which material will make the best blackout blinds / curtains?

It's really sunny today. Which is the best suntan cream? (Can be tested on UV beads)

How well do sunglasses block the light? Which type is the best?

What can children do when fair testing?

Ideas for activities

There are many different contexts in which children can carry out fair testing enquiries. Some suggestions for these are given in the Starting Points table on the previous two pages, and in each of the four activities described in detail later.

Developing scientific skills and understanding

A fair test can be a very satisfying type of science enquiry: children notice a difference in the way something behaves, identify a possible cause and carry out a test to find out whether their idea is correct. Purposeful tests will be motivating for children. There will not be so much incentive for them to carry out a test to find out something that they already know! Stimulating fair test enquiries that capture children's attention provide particularly good contexts for children to use and develop the skills of raising questions, planning, observing, measuring, recording, interpreting and presenting data. These skills provide a distinctive way for children to develop their understanding of scientific ideas. As children develop their skills, the depth and range of their understanding should also increase.

As in all types of scientific enquiry, children should become progressively more systematic and show more independence in the way they plan and carry out fair test enquiries. Their planning should develop from recognising when a test is fair to selecting which variables to change, measure and keep the same. Children should become increasingly sophisticated in the way they interpret their observations and develop more complex explanations using a range of evidence. Their evaluation of their enquiries should also show an increased awareness of the effectiveness of their working methods.

Enquiries of this type can involve qualitative observations that can be recorded in drawings, photos or notes, and quantitative data that can be presented in tables, bar charts or graphs. Younger children can make simple comparisons (e.g. the car on the steepest slope went furthest) and find ways of communicating these comparisons (e.g. paper strips to show how far the car went, presented as a simple bar graph). Older children will have opportunities to use more complex ways of presenting data. These will include constructing line graphs, where they can plot two continuous variables against each other (e.g. depth of planting and time taken for shoot to appear), read between the marked points, consider how the graph might continue and draw conclusions about how the variables are connected.

The grid on page 142 shows the progression of skills that children use when carrying out fair tests. You can use the grid to ensure that there is sufficient challenge in the fair testing enquiries that you plan.

Encouraging talk and questioning

Children can be very good at noticing differences and asking why. Help them to plan for fair testing by turning 'why' questions into 'how' or 'what does' questions.

You want to know why Jake's spinner flies better than yours. I wonder what makes a difference?

They need to decide what variable they will test and what outcome they will observe. Give them time to talk to each other to check that they are only changing one variable.

Jake's spinner is made of thicker card than yours, and he's taller than you so he launched his higher up. Do you think that might make a difference? What do you need to keep the same? Talk to each other about your ideas.

Encourage them to talk about how to measure the effect and record their results.

How will you check how quickly it spins? Do you need a table for the results?

Encourage children to talk about their observations and look for evidence.

The spinner with the middle sized wing spun most. You think it might be something to do with air resistance. How can you find out?

Encourage the children to think about how fair their test was and whether their results are reliable. They can make decisions about how to record and communicate their findings, and raise new questions to investigate.

What are the possible outcomes?

Fair test activities will lead to different kinds of outcomes that will provide rich assessment evidence:

> children planning and carrying out fair tests systematically

> the development of scientific understanding about concepts such as forces and properties of materials

> children being able to think, talk and write about the skills that they have used to identify cause and effect

> explanations that link the causal relationship they have identified to their prior scientific knowledge.

Fair Testing: Skills Progression Grid

	Plan	**Do**	**Review**
Foundation	• I am curious about how things behave • With help, I ask questions about things I can test • I talk about my ideas for testing how things behave	• I use my senses to look closely at how things behave • I carry out simple tests • I make simple records of what I notice (with help where necessary) • I use simple equipment to observe and record	• I talk about what I have done and what I noticed • I talk about whether something makes a difference
Early primary	• I ask questions about why and how • With help, I notice links between cause and effect • With help, I identify simple variables to change and measure	• I use non-standard units and simple equipment to record data • I record in words or pictures, or in simple prepared formats such as tables and tally charts	• I interpret and talk about my data • I begin to use simple scientific language to identify and describe simple causal relationships • With help, I can say if my test was fair • I say if the relationship was what I expected
Middle primary	• I talk about links between cause and effect and (with help) pose a fair test question • I help to plan a fair test • I decide what data to collect • I decide what equipment to use and how to make observations	• I use a range of equipment to collect data using standard measures • I make records using tables and bar charts • I begin to use and interpret data collected through dataloggers	• I draw simple conclusions from my fair tests • I talk about, and explain, simple causal relationships using some scientific language • I suggest ways that I can improve my fair tests
Late primary	• I recognise when variables need to be controlled and when a fair test is the best way to answer my question • I plan a fair test, selecting the most suitable variables to measure, change and keep the same • I decide what equipment to use to make my measurements as accurate as possible	• I use equipment accurately to collect observations • I record data appropriately and accurately • I present data in line graphs • I identify causal relationships	• I draw valid conclusions based on the data • I recognise the significance of the results of fair tests • I talk about and explain causal relationships using scientific knowledge and understanding • I evaluate the effectiveness of my fair testing, recognising variables that were difficult to control

WASHING DAY

Getting clothes clean can be a rich context for fair testing. Children's early enquiries involve observing and exploring the world without attempting to control the factors involved. At this stage, children can develop simple ideas about why it helps to keep some things the same when they are investigating their ideas. By exaggerating you can help them to see the problems involved when things are not kept the same (e.g. by using lots of soap on one thing and a tiny amount on another, or a big patch of dirt on one thing and a tiny spot on the other). Don't be concerned if things are not kept precisely the same, since this could detract from the experience that you want the children to have.

Give children time to explore what happens when things are washed. Encourage children to talk and think about what they did and what made a difference to what happens. By doing this you provide an opportunity to help the children begin to understand the need for fairness when they carry out their enquiries.

Health and Safety Notes
- Do not use any toxic cleaning products. Use mild washing products such as hand soap or hand-washing detergents. If you wish to investigate the differences between washing powders it is best to handle these yourself (wear gloves) or use a washing machine. Ensure that water is at a safe temperature.

Getting started

You can build on children's spontaneous observations and questions

Both indoor and outdoor play will provide plenty of opportunities to investigate getting things clean.

I've got paint on my T-shirt!

I ran into a puddle and my socks are all dirty!

We were chasing the ball and fell over. My trousers have got lots of mud all over them.

You can ask questions to focus their observations

Use your questions to work towards things that can be explored using simple tests.

Have you seen clothes being washed at home?

How do you think we can get the clothes clean?

What might help us?

You can provide your own starting points

You can provide very natural starting points, by contriving an accident where something gets dirty in the classroom or outside play area.

Oh no! I knocked my coffee over and mopped it up with a towel, and now the towel has gone brown.

My dog jumped up on me just as I was leaving for school this morning. Look at the top I was wearing! How am I going to get it clean?

It was prize giving day and Jake was going to get a special prize. He was wearing his very best T-shirt. He was very happy. Hop, skip, jump, SPLOSH! Oh no! How was he going to get clean again? Fortunately.......

WHAT CAN CHILDREN DO?

IDEAS FOR ACTIVITIES

Children can:

> explore washing things by hand and by machine
> investigate what makes a difference to getting things clean, such as different soaps, temperature of the water, leaving to soak, rubbing, type of material, type of stain and whether the stain is wet or dry
> find out what happens when brightly coloured things are washed
> find out what is the best way to get things dry (e.g. sunshine, over a radiator, windy day)
> take pictures of the stains before and after they have been cleaned, or make videos of how to clean the clothes
> make drawings of what they did and use these to make a wall display, adding information to it when new things are found out about washing clothes
> make an indoor washing line and share what happened by hanging the things that they have tried to clean on the line. With help, information/labels can be added to the line
> make up stories about how things got dirty and then how they were cleaned again
> visit a laundrette.

DEVELOPING SKILLS AND UNDERSTANDING

Give children lots of opportunities to:

> look carefully at what happens to the fabric, the water, the soap, and talk about what they can see
> make a visual record of their observations in drawings or photographs
> think about why it helps to keep some things the same when they are investigating
> talk about which were the best ways of getting things clean and how they know
> make connections between what they did to the fabric and what happened
> develop and use key vocabulary (e.g. fair, keep the same, change, rub, rinse, wash, dirty, clean, dry, fabric).

Encouraging talk and questioning

Encourage the children to think carefully about how they get things clean. You can ask questions to direct their observations and help them plan what to do.

> *Who has seen clothes being washed at home? How did they get washed?*
>
> *What can we do with this shirt to get it clean again? Talk to your partner.*

Give them time to explore with a partner and encourage them to share with each other what they see.

> *Here are some cloths with dirt on them. How do you think you can get them clean? Try some different ideas and look closely at what happens. Talk to your partner about what you can see.*
>
> *You can use warm water or cold water. Which will you choose?*
>
> *How can we decide which is the best way to get them clean? Is it OK if I use lots of soap on this one and a tiny bit on this? What do you think?*

When they have finished encourage them to talk about what they have found out.

> *What was the best way to get them clean? Talk to your partner about what you found out.*

Encourage them to think about new questions.

> *I've got a new question. I've got coffee stains on my T-shirt, not mud. I wonder if that makes a difference?*
>
> *I've washed the towel, but it's still dirty. What do you think we should do?*
>
> *Do you have anything you would like to ask?*

What are the possible outcomes?

Washing clothes leads to different kinds of outcomes

These can provide rich assessment evidence of their developing skills and understanding.

For example:

> what they say to each other, and you, about what happens when they try to get things clean and dry

> how carefully they observe (e.g. changes to the stain, the colour of the water, how long they had to rub for)

> the connections that they begin to make between what they did and what happened (e.g. the cloth in the warm water was cleaner than the one in the cold water)

> what they say about trying to keep things the same

> their drawings and photographs and any annotations that are added (generally with help)

> how well they focus on their investigations and the ideas that they suggest

> the ideas that they contribute to information boards, classroom displays or play area

> the stories they create (with help)

> what they tell you about the things that they found out and what they might do next.

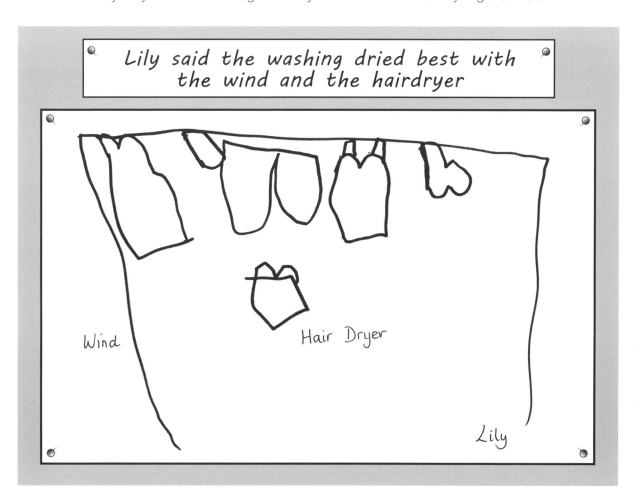

Lily said the washing dried best with the wind and the hairdryer

Wind   Hair Dryer   Lily

Questions that can lead to other types of enquiry

My grandad uses stuff in a bottle to wash his clothes. Are there lots of ways to get clothes clean?

What do you do if you've got lots and lots of clothes to clean?

Have there always been washing machines?

What happens in a dry cleaners? Do they wash clothes?

Can we make a clothes cleaning place (laundry room) in our classroom? How will we wash all the different things?

How can you add challenge?

Children can be encouraged to:

> compare what they found with what they expected

> observe more systematically, looking for changes

> with support, collect data about the things that they did (e.g. how much water, number of rubs, whether they used soap)

> decide for themselves what to do.

CAN WE HEAR THE TEACHER'S WHISTLE?

Listening for the teacher's whistle (or some other sound that marks the end of playtime) uses a familiar context for looking at fair testing. Children already recognise the sound and know that that they can hear it. However they will probably not have thought about the connection between sound and hearing.

A range of factors might affect how well they can hear the sound, for example, whether they are wearing a hood, how hard they blow the whistle, which way they are standing, the direction of the wind or distance from the whistle. Children doing this activity may be at the early stages of developing their understanding of the need for fair tests, therefore it is important not to over-complicate the factors being considered or being controlled. By exploring some simple factors, we can help children to develop the concept of only changing one thing at a time in order to make the tests fair. We can also lay the foundation for later work on sound production, the nature of sound and how sound travels.

> ### *Health and Safety Notes*
> - *Follow your school's guidelines for working out of doors. If whistles or other blown instruments need to be used by more than one child, they will need cleaning with an appropriate sterilising fluid (e.g. Milton) between uses. Be sensitive to any children who have hearing impairments.*

Getting started

You can build on children's spontaneous observations and questions

The end of playtime is a golden opportunity for capturing children's ideas, assuming that a whistle is blown.

> *I didn't hear the whistle blow. Did you hear it?*
>
> *We didn't hear the whistle today because it was windy.*

You can ask questions to focus their observations

Use your questions to lead towards ideas that can be investigated using fair tests.

> *Did everybody hear the whistle? Do we all hear the same things?*
>
> *Does it matter where you stand in the playground? Will everybody be able to hear the whistle?*
>
> *Do you think the wind makes a difference to what we hear?*

You can provide your own starting points

You can make an observation that raises a question, or use stories.

> *When I blow the whistle at playtime, some children don't seem to hear it. I wonder why that is?*
>
> *I've been given a new whistle, but I'm not sure that I like it. I think we can hear the old one better. What do you think?*
>
> *The new teacher in class 3 says that in her old school they use a bell at the end of playtime. Do you think a bell will be better than a whistle?*

> *Tibby's dad has got a new job, he also has a problem. He has to work during the night and that means he has to sleep during the day. They live near the football ground and on Saturday her dad can't sleep because of the referee's whistle. Then Tibby has an idea.......*

WHAT CAN CHILDREN DO?

IDEAS FOR ACTIVITIES

Children can:

> talk to each other about what makes a difference to how well they can hear a whistle when it is blown
> go outside and investigate their ideas, such as whether the wind is blowing, the wind direction, the amount of background noise, or whether it has been raining
> go outside and investigate their ideas, such as wearing a hood, how hard they blow the whistle, or distance from the whistle
> find out if the type of whistle makes a difference to what they hear (e.g. make their own paper straw whistles and explore whistles of varying pitch)
> investigate the best place for the teacher to stand to blow the whistle or ring the bell for the end of playtime
> investigate the best ways of stopping sound
> with help, create some guidance for teachers to make sure that children can hear the whistle or bell.

DEVELOPING SKILLS AND UNDERSTANDING

Give children lots of opportunities to:

> raise questions based on their own observations of what happens when whistles are blown
> use their experiences to suggest what they might do to find out more and how they might do it (e.g. count how many children can hear the whistle, or how far away they can stand and still hear it)
> with support, talk and think about what things they will try to keep the same to make their investigation fair
> record their observations in a simple picture, table, tally or bar chart
> talk with each other about what they found out themselves or learned from other children's results
> with help, identify straightforward patterns in the data
> begin to link cause and effect in their explanations (e.g. we can't hear the sound so well if we stand round the corner of the building because sound can't get round the corner)
> develop and use key vocabulary (e.g. fair, explain, change, listen, sound, noise, hear, distance, travel).

Encouraging talk and questioning

Give children time to talk together about what they know about hearing things.

When do you find it difficult to hear things? Share your ideas.

I think that children standing with their backs to me don't hear the whistle very well. Do you think I am right? Talk to your partner about your ideas.

Encourage them to think and talk about how to find out. A period of initial exploration will help them to do this.

Why don't we divide into groups and go to different places to listen? Where do you think will be the best place to hear the whistle?

Let's go outside with all the different whistles that we have made. How will we find out which we can hear best?

Minelli says that she can't hear very well when she has her hood up. Do you think that's true for everyone? What can we do to check?

When they have finished, encourage them to talk about what they have found out.

What happened when you stood in different places to listen for the whistle?

Talk together in your groups to see if you can work out what makes a difference to what we hear. Have you all found the same thing?

Encourage children to raise more questions.

I've thought of another question. If we use a bell will we hear it better?

My mother doesn't like lots of noise. What do you think she might do?

What questions do you have?

What are the possible outcomes?

Testing how we hear whistles leads to different kinds of outcomes

These can provide rich assessment evidence of their developing skills and understanding.

For example:

> what they say to each other, and you, about what happens when they listen for the whistle

> what they observe about when and how they can hear the whistle

> their pictures or tables to show the best way to hear the whistle

> the connections they make between what they did and what they noticed

> the advice they give about where the teacher should stand to blow the whistle

> what they say about whether the tests they did were fair

> what they tell you about the things that they have found out and what they might do next.

Seb's group wondered if their results would be different on a windy day

We can hear the whistle
tohen   beot neccor the

Questions that can lead to other types of enquiry

Questions that children may ask (or you could ask them)

Where in the school do our instruments sound the loudest? How can we play them without disturbing other classes?

How does a whistle work?

I heard birds whistling when I walked to school. Will they still be whistling on my way home?

My uncle has a hearing aid. I wonder what it's for?

People say that bats have very special ears but I'm not sure why. Where can I find out more?

Can all animals hear? Are there some animals that don't hear? Does it matter if some of them can't hear? How am I going to find out?

How can you add challenge?

Children can be encouraged to:

> suggest more questions about hearing that they could investigate

> test different materials to find out which is best at stopping the sound

> make their own suggestions about how to make sure that tests are fair.

CONSUMER TESTING (TOOTHPASTE)

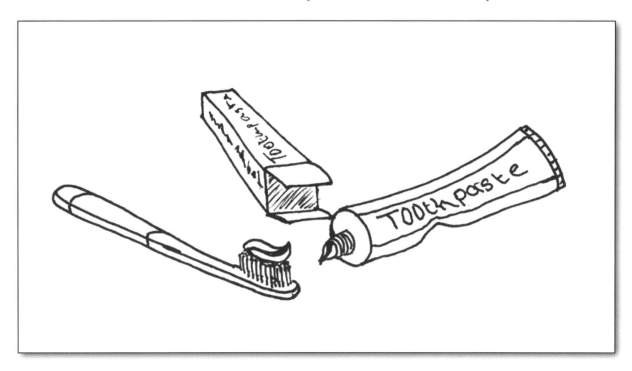

Consumer tests provide a rich source of ideas for enquiries involving fair testing. Most manufacturers of consumer goods spend a lot of time researching and developing their products. Investigating products allows manufacturers' claims and ratings to be tested. It also provides an opportunity to introduce the idea of looking critically at data and how they are used. Is the claim justified? How were the data obtained?

This example focuses on toothpaste. Like many other product manufacturers, toothpaste companies make claims about their toothpaste. A period of research using the packaging of toothpaste and toothpaste advertisements, and some time spent exploring the properties of toothpaste, would be a useful lead in to this activity. The framework for this activity can be used for other fair test enquiries based on product testing (e.g. which nappy soaks up most water, or which carrier bag is the strongest).

Health and Safety Notes
- *Most tests, including those using homemade toothpaste, should not be carried out on children's own teeth. Use stains on egg shells, ceramic tiles or white plates.*

Getting started

You can build on children's spontaneous observations and questions

You might want to alert children to the fact that you are going to investigate toothpaste and encourage them to look for ideas to investigate.

We bought the new toothpaste that was advertised on the television. It tastes great. I think it will be better than my old toothpaste.

Eating the red sweets at playtime made our teeth go bright red.

You can ask questions to focus their observations

Use questions that lead children towards the need for fair testing.

How can we find out if the new toothpaste is better? What do you think we mean by better?

What do you need to do to get rid of the red on your teeth? If you need to use toothpaste, does it matter which you use?

When the dental nurse came into school she got you to use one type of toothpaste to get the disclosing tablet off your teeth. But it took ages. I wonder if any other toothpaste would be quicker?

You can provide your own starting points

You can make an observation that raises a question.

Look at this advert for toothpaste. What do you think about what it says? Do you think it's all true? How can we find out if what they say is correct?

Could you create your own advert for a new toothpaste? What would you say? You can't just tell lies about it! That means you will have to do some tests first.

A new dentist has opened in the town. Children like this dentist because she always gives them interesting toothpaste to try. She wonders what is the best toothpaste to use. Can you help her?

WHAT CAN CHILDREN DO?

IDEAS FOR ACTIVITIES

Children can:

> talk to each other to identify the main properties of toothpaste (e.g. cleaning power, texture, taste)

> work together to explore toothpaste boxes and adverts to identify the main claims about toothpaste, then share the different claims across the class and use jig-sawing to draw together what they have found

> make and test their own toothpaste, using ingredients that they have chosen for themselves or using varying proportions of ingredients that you have provided (e.g. baking soda, glycerine, cornflour, salt, water, colouring and flavouring)

> see if there are any links between their data and people's favourite toothpastes

> compare their own toothpaste with commercially manufactured toothpaste

> test other dental products such as dental disclosing tablets

> research the history of teeth cleaning and test the various methods

> create adverts making claims based on their own research. How do they compare with the manufacturers' adverts?

> create packaging for their own toothpaste.

DEVELOPING SKILLS AND UNDERSTANDING

Give children lots of opportunities to:

> explore and talk about the product that they will be investigating

> decide if they should carry out a fair test and plan how they will make the test fair

> observe, measure and record the data in an appropriate scientific way (e.g. a chart or table)

> identify straightforward patterns and trends in their results

> describe and explain what they found out

> evaluate what they did (e.g. Did we know which thing we were changing and what to keep the same? Did we collect the data carefully?)

> develop and use key vocabulary (e.g. fair test, product, consumer testing, variable (factor), control, change, results, data).

Encouraging talk and questioning

Encourage the children to look closely at the different claims made about toothpaste. You can ask questions to help them discuss and plan how they will carry out their enquiries and whether fair tests are necessary. They will need to compare different toothpastes.

The toothpaste I use doesn't stay on the brush very well. When I clean my teeth most of the toothpaste ends up in the sink! Is your toothpaste any better than mine?

What do the toothpaste manufacturers say that the toothpaste will do? Work in your group and see if you can make a list.

Encourage children to think about the best way to answer their questions.

How can you find out if what the manufacturers of toothpaste say is right? Put a star by the side of things that you can investigate by doing a fair test.

Are there other things that they say, like 'new tangy flavour 'or 'mintier than ever' that you have to investigate in a different way, such as doing some research? How will you make sure that your tests are fair?

After they have finished investigating you can encourage children to talk about their results.

Work with a partner to look at what you have recorded. Try to decide if you have any information that will help you to grade the toothpaste from good to poor, and give them a star rating.

Find another pair and compare your grades.

What do you think about those adverts now you have done some testing? Are they accurate? Are they fair? Talk together about what you think.

You can encourage them to raise more questions.

I've got a question. If we had used a different kind of toothbrush would that have made any difference to our results? Look at what you found out.

Do you have any questions that you would like to answer?

What are the possible outcomes?

Carrying out fair tests linked to products leads to different kinds of outcomes

These can provide rich assessment evidence of their developing skills and understanding.

For example:

> what they say to each other, and you, about the claims that are made about toothpaste and how these claims can be tested

> the notes and other records they make about their research into claims about toothpaste

> the suggestions that they make for how they can carry out fair test investigations on toothpaste and the way the tests are carried out

> the way that they record the data they collect and analyse the results

> the ways that they suggest their tests can be modified in the light of outcomes and questions that they raise

> the records of how they compared commercially made and homemade toothpaste

> their posters and other ways of communicating their findings

> their own toothpaste packaging

> their evaluation of what they have done.

Anna's group said their data showed that homemade toothpaste was as good as some shop bought ones

Anna	Plaque + Stain Remover	Smell	Stay on Brush	Colour	Taste
Home made - Anna	2 scrubs	5	1 Shake only	1	Too Salty
Home made Dad	8 scrubs	4	5 shakes	4 green	Too Salty
Ben 10	Did not Remove Stain	3	5 Shakes	5 Blue	4
Euccyl Powder	6 Scrubs	3	most comes off with 1 Shake only	5 Pink	1
ARM + Hammer Freshmint Gel	7 scrubs	5	2 shakes	2 green	1 'Brity'
Colgate Cavity Protection	Did not Remove Stain	5	3 shakes	1 Plain white	5 Best taste
Aqua fresh	15 scrubs	1	1 shakes	4 Stripey	3 memtbl
Colgate	27 scrubs	2	7 shake	2	2

Questions that can lead to other types of enquiry

Questions that children may ask (or you could ask them)

How is toothpaste made in factories?

Someone said cola damages teeth? If we put an egg in cola how will it change over time?

I wonder which are the best ways of cleaning teeth? How did people manage to clean their teeth before we had toothpaste?

Which are people's favourite toothpastes and why?

Why do they put fluoride in toothpaste? Is fluoride always good for you?

How can you add challenge?

Children can be encouraged to:

> make their own plans and carry out a series of fair tests on different aspects of the toothpaste

> make their own decisions about how to present their data

> identify new questions to be answered

> think about issues relating to science and advertising, such as whether all claims are testable or justified.

ONE POTATO, TWO POTATO

Growing things in schools provides rich opportunities for children to carry out different types of science enquiries. Growing potatoes is extremely easy and provides a real-life context for fair testing. Potatoes are often grown in schools, but the opportunity for fair testing may not be exploited.

Several factors can have a big influence on the yield from growing potatoes, including what variety is grown, amount of fertiliser and amount of water. Once children start thinking about the factors that might influence how potatoes grow, they can generate a range of questions and set up a wide variety of tests. Fair testing is needed to identify which variables are the most important and decide which is the best way to grow the potatoes.

> ### *Health and Safety Notes*
> * *Follow the school's guidelines for working out of doors. Ensure that all tools are suitable for the children involved and are handled, and carried, with care. Demonstrate how to use and carry tools if children are inexperienced.*
> * *Do not let children use any pesticides or undiluted fertilisers. Any part of a potato or potato plant which is green is poisonous, as are the flowers.*
> * *Children should wash their hands after working outdoors or handling plants and growing medium.*

Getting started

You can build on children's spontaneous observations and questions

You may want to alert children to the fact they are going to be growing potatoes and ask them to think about how they are grown.

> *Nan hasn't got many potatoes on her allotment this year. She's not sure why.*
>
> *The potatoes in this tub seem to be growing better than the others.*

You can ask questions to focus their observations

Use questions that lead towards the need for fair testing.

> *How can we find out what happened with Nan's potatoes?*
>
> *Is there any difference in the way that the potatoes were grown in the different tubs?*

You can provide your own starting points

You can make an observation that raises a question.

> *We're going to grow potatoes in school this year. Someone told me that fertiliser will help them to grow well. How can we find out?*
>
> *When we grew potatoes last year my class thought that earthing up made a big difference to how they grew. I wonder if that's right. How do you think we can find out?*

You could start with a letter from a local farmer or gardener who has a question about growing potatoes. For example:

> *I've been told that the soil round here isn't very good for growing potatoes. What do you think? Can you help me find out?*
>
> *Fertiliser is really expensive. Do I really have to use it to grow my potatoes?*
>
> *I'm planning to grow potatoes every year and keep a record of how they grow. I want to find out the best way to grow them. Can you help me?*

WHAT CAN CHILDREN DO?

IDEAS FOR ACTIVITIES

Children can:

> grow some potatoes in tubs, bags or in the school garden
> talk to each other about what makes a difference to how well potatoes grow
> investigate their ideas about growing conditions such as whether fertiliser is used, the amount of water they get, temperature, using fleece to warm the soil, depth of planting, and earthing up
> investigate other ideas, such as using different types of potato, using half or whole potatoes, and chitting (allowing the potatoes to sprout) before planting
> investigate the best way to store potatoes
> plan how to carry out their investigations and how to gather and record data
> talk to a farmer or gardener about the best way to grow potatoes then write a report for them
> produce a guide to growing potatoes with photographs, drawings and diagrams.

DEVELOPING SKILLS AND UNDERSTANDING

Give children lots of opportunities to:

> ask questions about how potatoes grow
> carry out regular observations and talk about them to each other
> collect data by measuring accurately, record the data in a tally chart or table, and convert the data into a graph
> identify patterns in the sets of data and talk to each other about these patterns
> use their scientific knowledge about growing things to draw straightforward conclusions about cause and effect
> evaluate how effective their investigation was and how they might improve it (e.g. Did we measure accurately? Did we take into account other factors that might have made a difference?)
> use and develop key vocabulary (e.g. fair test, variable (factor), change, control, measure, tuber, root, fertiliser, growth, temperature).

Encouraging talk and questioning

Encourage children to explore and talk about what they know about growing things.

Who has grown potatoes at home? Did you notice anything about what helped them to grow?

I'm going to give you five minutes in your groups to think of anything you know about growing things. Let's share our ideas. Now decide what questions you have about how we should grow the potatoes.

You can encourage children to talk to each other about the questions and ideas that they raise about growing potatoes.

How can we answer your questions?

What do we need to measure and record?

How long will we need to collect data?

How do you think we can make the test fair?

What things should we change or keep the same?

When children have finished investigating, encourage them to talk together about what they have found.

Find another group and talk together about what you have recorded. What was the same about your data? What was different?

Can you think of any reasons why different groups might have different data?

Encourage them to raise new questions.

Now you have thought about the data, work in new groups of four to see if you can think of new questions about growing things that we can explore. Add them to the question board.

We're going to produce a guide to growing potatoes. Do you have all the information that you need? Are there more questions that you need to answer first?

What are the possible outcomes?

Carrying out fair tests by growing potatoes leads to different kinds of outcomes

These can provide rich assessment evidence of their developing skills and understanding.

For example:

> what they say to each other, and you, about growing potatoes and how they grow

> the ideas that they have about what tests to carry out

> the plans that they make for fair testing

> the ways that they gather data and talk about it

> the ways that they decide to record their data

> how they identify and describe the results

> the ways that they use data from other sources to help them learn

> the ideas that they share about growing potatoes and the tests they carry out

> the graphs or charts that they create

> the letters or guidance that they produce

> the way that they evaluate what they have done and the ideas they offer for how to improve their fair testing.

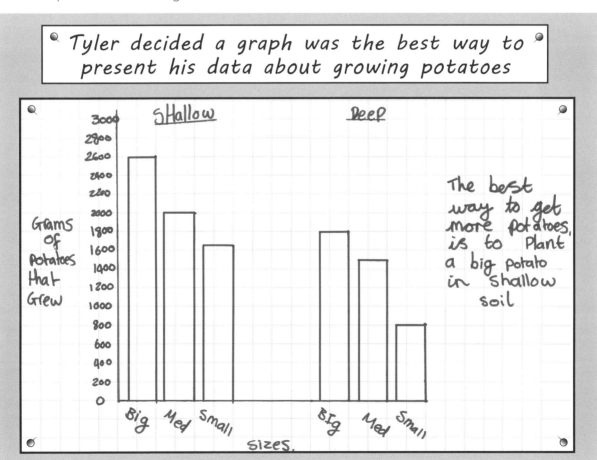

Tyler decided a graph was the best way to present his data about growing potatoes

Questions that can lead to other types of enquiry

Questions that children may ask (or you could ask them)

I know that chips and crisps are made from potatoes, but I wonder if any other foods are made from them?

Do all the different types of potatoes taste the same? How can I find my favourite?

How do potatoes change if we keep them for a long time?

What do other people say is the best way to grow potatoes?

What diseases can potatoes get?

What was the Irish potato famine, and how was it caused?

Are any other plants related to potatoes? What are they and can you eat them too?

Where did potatoes come from originally?

How can you add challenge?

Children can be encouraged to:

> be more systematic and precise in how they collect data

> take account of a greater range of variables, recognising which are most significant

> write an article for a local newspaper about growing potatoes

> recognise anomalies or inconsistencies in their data and try to explain them.

References & Bibliography

ASE (2011) *Be safe*, 4th Edition. Hatfield: Association for Science Education.

British Science Association (undated) *CREST Star Investigators Award Scheme*. London: British Science Association.

Carle, E. (1994) *The very hungry caterpillar*. London: Penguin.

Driver, R., Guesne, E. and Tiberghien, A. (Eds.) (1985) *Children's ideas in science*. Maidenhead: Open University.

Goldsworthy, A., and Feasey, R. (1997) *Making sense of primary science investigations*. Hatfield: Association for Science Education.

Goldsworthy, A., Watson, R. and Wood-Robinson, V. (1998) Sometimes it's not fair! *Primary Science Review*, May / June, 15-17.

Goldsworthy, A., Watson, R. and Wood-Robinson, V. (2000) *Investigations: developing understanding*. Hatfield: Association for Science Education.

Haigh, A. (2010) *The art of creative teaching: primary science*. Harlow: Pearson.

Harlen, W. (2001) *Primary science: taking the plunge*, 2nd Edition. Portsmouth: Heinemann.

Harlen, W. (2009) *The teaching of science in primary schools*, 5th Edition. London: Routledge.

Loxley, P., Dawes, L., Nicholls, L. and Dore, B. (2010) *Teaching primary science*. Harlow: Pearson.

Naylor, B. and Naylor, S. (2010) *Science questions* (CD-ROM). Sandbach: Millgate House Education.

Naylor, S. and Keogh, B. with Goldsworthy, A. (2004) *Active assessment: thinking, learning and assessment in science*. Chiswick: David Fulton/Sandbach: Millgate House Education.

Rich, D., Casanova, D., Dixon, A., Drummond, M.J., Durrant, A. and Myer, C. (2005) *First hand experience: what matters to children*. Suffolk: Rich Learning Opportunities.

Rich, D., Drummond, M.J. and Myer, C. (2008) *Learning: what matters to children*. Suffolk: Rich Learning Opportunities.

Watson, R., Goldsworthy, A. and Wood-Robinson, V. (1998) *AKSIS project second interim report to the QCA*. London: Kings College.

Weaver, G. (2008) *Made you look, made you think, made you talk*. Sandbach: Millgate House Education.